OPTIONS TRADING STRATEGIES

The Only Guide on Advanced
Day, Swing and Binary Strategies
You Need to Trade in Stock
Market, Start Now Your Journey
to Become a Professional Trader
(Includes Graphs).

HENRY LIVING

Table of Contents

Introduction

If you enjoy trading, love the stock market, and are passionate about options trading, then you can get rich while doing what you love. The chapters in this book will guide you through this journey. You will learn about the strategies that have huge potential, as well as the most profitable options you should focus on.

The best thing to do to get started is to buy some calls and puts on index funds. Start small, let your account grow, and accept that you will have some losses along the way. That is the reality when you decide to work with this type of investment or business – there is a risk for losses along the way. But that does not mean that losses will be a constant thing. If you play your cards right, really study the market and make sound decisions – you are bound to rebound from your losses and start gaining profits. Risk is in everything that we do, and it all just varies depending on how we mitigate these risks and make them work to our advantage. We cannot predict how the market will fare daily, stock prices are affected by a lot of factors, and most of them are things we cannot control, that is one of the things that you need to keep in mind.

When you are ready to start making some money with options and you want to learn the right way to do it to reduce your risks and make some money, then take the time to look through this guidebook to help you get started.

Chapter 1

INTRODUCTION TO OPTION TRADING STRATEGIES

Options trading in the realm of the stock market has a great deal of pay potential, and it is loaded with economic advantages if you pick and pursue the right strategy. There are numerous option trading strategies that a speculator can select from. Contingent upon the impression you have about the heading of the stock price movement, you can choose an options strategy.

When you are ignorant regarding the movement of the underlying stock price, then you should pick a neutral options trading strategy which is otherwise called a non-directional trading strategy. The potential profit relies upon the volatility of the underlying stock price. Some regular models of neutral trading strategies are straddle and butterfly.

There are numerous online projects and instructional classes that will show you how to trade options and pick the right strategy that would accommodate your objectives and trading style.

You ought to recollect that options are very flexible trading instruments. With such extraordinary adaptability, this is the place numerous individuals fail to understand the situation. They imagine that the more complex an options trading strategy is, the more effective it tends to be. Truth be told it very well may be the inverse. The more complex the plan, the more open you could be to hazard while in the meantime restricting profit potential.

Similarly, as with any strategy you utilize with your options trading business and approach it with deference. Try not to trade live until the point when you have given it a decent test using a training account. At precisely that point should you consider running with it using your real money.

When figuring out how to trade options, it is continuously prudent to utilize chance capital when purchasing with real money. This implies using money that you can stand to lose on the off chance that you have trades that conflict with you. There you go that contacts the surface of options trading strategies. You will need to take in more and after that select a plan to trade your options utilizing a test account. From that point who knows.

Keep in mind forget not to give things a chance to escape hand if you are taking in another strategy trade with one contract at a time. If you go over the edge, you will before long end up crazy and headed towards fiasco. Options trading isn't a race. You have time on your side, and you should capitalize on it. The market will at present be here tomorrow.

Regardless of what you do in life, there is dependably a first day. Strolling as an infant, driving a vehicle, or starting another employment all fall into this class. This is valid for beginner's options trading in the stock market too. Regardless of whether you have encountered trading stocks you probably won't know the contrast between a call and a put; don't get stressed because this wouldn't prompt a pop test. What will happen is that we will see options trading for beginners and give you a portion of the fundamentals to kick you off. If you have never been presented to options trading, welcome to your first day!

Chapter 2
HOW TO CHOOSE THE BEST OPTIONS TRADING STRATEGY

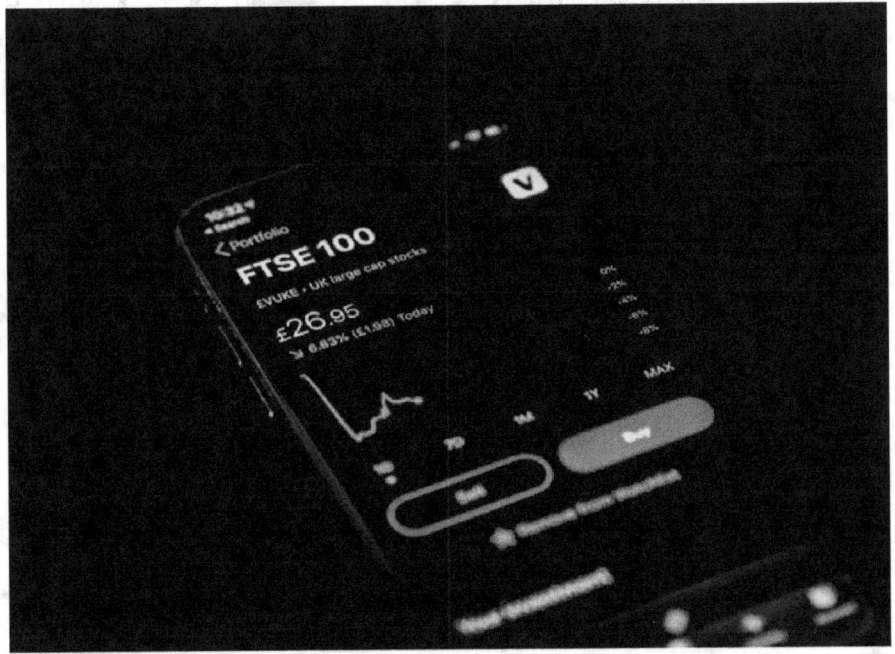

The enchantment of options trading is that it takes into account an assortment of strategies to be coordinated with various stock trading methods of insight. Each technique has an alternate benefit and hazard resilience level and utilizing a variety of plans can zest up a portfolio in all respects pleasantly! In this part, I will plot four unique stock trading strategies, and how they can be coordinated with options trading strategies that you can apply to your portfolio. The fundamental idea is to concentrate on an underlying stock trading technique initially, and afterward add noteworthy influence and capacity to the trade by utilizing options.

The most significant factor while considering each of these strategies is the idea of time decay. The estimation of any option decreases after some time, until the day the option terminates. This idea can be the significant adversary of any options trade, eating into its benefits, or it very well may be the way to fruitful and productive option trading.

Initially, which strategy should you use?

There are commonly four unique strategies utilized by stock traders, each of which has suggestions when connected to options:

POSITION TRADING

Merchants purchase a stock and hold it for extended time frames, in light of the right essentials of the organization. They will regularly trust that a stock will reach high esteem, and afterward watch for institutional or insider buying before making a move. As the stock cost increases, they pay a unique mind to different buyers to venture in and move the cost considerably further.

PROPER OPTION STRATEGY

Buying calls and puts aren't proper, because you pay substantial premiums for time esteem, the majority of which could be cleared out after some time even as the stock gains in cost. Time decay is your adversary.

Selling canvassed calls each month in the option cycle on the stock you already claim can altogether diminish the cost you paid for the stock in the first trade. Regardless of whether the stock goes down, you can, in any case, turn out a champ!

MOMENTUM OR TREND TRADING

When a stock has clarified move or breakout, the Momentum traders venture in and ride the share up along a pattern to its first real inversion. They want to make shorter-term benefits from a rapid move in the cost. Holding periods run from about a month and a half to a half year.

FITTING OPTION STRATEGY

Buying calls and puts aren't fitting, since you pay vast premiums for time esteem, the vast majority of which will be cleared out after some time even as the stock gains in cost. Time decay is your adversary with Momentum Trading unless you have an excellent and quick-moving pattern.

Selling Credit Spreads is a decent technique, and in reality can be entirely beneficial, because as you sell spreads on the contrary leg from the stock's course of momentum (for example selling put acknowledge spreads in stock for an emphatically bullish pattern), you can repeatedly buy back the ranges for least expense and sell another range nearer in. This methodology can quickly return a 10-15% benefit every month. Time decay is your clear-cut advantage for trading this technique.

Selling Naked Puts is a conventional technique and can be much more beneficial than selling credit spreads. Nonetheless, it leaves you a place of conceivably purchasing a lot of stock if the trade conflicts with you, thus your broker expects you to have a lot of edges.

SWING TRADING

Swing Traders buy and sell swings or motions inside a pattern. Holding times are from somewhere in the range of two and ten days. This is a shorter-term trading system that is more reliant on the profile heading than it is on essentials or specific indicators.

PROPER OPTION STRATEGY

If you have aced the aptitude of distinguishing inversions or swings inside a pattern, and expertise to design a leave system, you will almost certainly begin buying calls and puts, or DITM options, which will take you to real benefits! With Swing Trading, holding times are short (2-10 days) thus you limit the impact of your chief foe, time decay.

DAY TRADING

Informal investors center around the many little moves that occur amid the trading day, mostly appeared by candle designs. This procedure has a broker's necessity of at least $25,000 to qualify, which thumps out numerous tenderfoots.

BINARY OPTIONS TRADING STRATEGIES

Having a very much made double choices trading technique is a benefit for brokers. It will assist them with overcoming any unforeseen occasions on the money related market. The area of dual alternatives is volatile; thus, it is hard to have a one of a kind technique that will fit in all circumstances. Anyway, the merchant can pursue specific guidelines that will control him all through his trading venture, and that may expand his profits.

OBSERVING THE FINANCIAL MARKET

Observing the money related market is a standout amongst the most significant techniques every merchant ought to embrace while talking about trading online. Also, tracking the patterns the benefits are following is a primordial component of an active exchange. The two instruments that can be utilized to watch out for the headings the benefits are moving in are:

SPECIALIZED ANALYSIS

Technical examination is a device which investigates past monetary value inclines to make estimates about the future patterns. It is an extremely productive procedure since it breaks down the interest and supply relating to a particular market. In like manner, from the information acquired, the Technical investigation can decide the heading the market will keep on following later on. The data produced by this investigation can genuinely change the round of the merchants.

FACTUAL ANALYSIS

Moreover, there is a measurable examination. It might appear to be troublesome at first look as only one out of every odd merchant has thought of measurements. Nonetheless, the merchant does not have to set out on complex computations as luckily; some business firms offer an administration which is known as the Daily Market Analysis. These are daily reports issued by experts that complete a profound examination of the whole market. The, for the most part, spread the overall execution of benefits, for example, stocks, files, monetary forms, and wares.

Dealers ought not to disregard the significance of checking the market as it is the way to boosting their productive exchanges.

PICK A TRADING TOOL AND PRACTICE

One standard procedure that can be utilized by dealers is known as Day Trading. This sort of trading is alluded to as an exchange which includes the buy and the closeout of stocks inside 24 hours. It is very prescribed as dealers utilizing this system can produce a vast volume of profits just by checking little value developments. To be fruitful with day trading here are a few hints:

SET AN ENTRY PRICE

In request to abstain from being excessively enthusiastic amid the exchange, it is advised that the brokers set a passage cost. Ravenousness might take over amid a trade that is, the merchant chooses to contribute considerably more than he arranged at first. This conduct can be as dangerous as your judgment is affected by feelings. This sort of behavior can convey the dealer to his misfortune. This is the reason it is imperative to set a passage cost to guarantee that the metal casing of the dealer won't meddle in his exchanges.

PURSUE THE INTRA-DAY TREND

The merchant ought to pursue the intra-day pattern. That is, the merchants will significantly diminish hazards when they exchange by following the pattern. Although the intra-day model will switch at a specific time, despite everything, it enables the dealers to produce a high benefit.

Track the exchanges made - All dealers should track their exhibition. Other than regardless of whether the time has come devouring, composing a rundown of the losing and winning trades will assist the brokers with knowing precisely what they did well and what they fouled up. This rundown will go about as a specific rule of the do's and don'ts of day trading dependent on their understanding.

CASH MANAGEMENT

While discussing Binary Options, it is critical to have decent cash for the executive's procedure. Generally, the broker will end up at the wrong end of the market. Indeed, it is inescapable to lose a few exchanges once in a while; this is the reason it is, much increasingly, essential to have decent cash. The board system will guarantee that the losing exchanges won't debilitate all the money contributed. Rather than going for winning every one of the transactions, the brokers should go for winding up with a huge benefit that will cover his underlying speculation. A thoroughly thought out system will contribute just 5% of the underlying capital. That is, if the underlying venture of the broker is $2000, the last ought not to provide more than $100 per exchange.

It requires a great deal of tolerance as trading just 5% of the capital will create low returns. It will extensively decrease the dangers of siring huge losses.

Online trading is ending up progressively well-known these days and draws in no small measure of dealers yearly. To be set up to face these heartless industry merchants need a procedure that will enable them to confront every single sudden possibility. The most significant component that brokers should remember is that time and tolerance are their best partners.

THE USE OF OPTIONS TRADING STRATEGIES

Do you have stresses concerning by what means will you diminish the dangers of your commitment to alternatives trading? Is it true that you are wishing to have lesser misfortune and higher benefit? Would you like to expand your assets and develop your prosperity rate? If your answer is 'yes,' all you need is a compelling and productive choices trading procedure. This will be such a significant amount of support for novices, specialists, and different dimensions of people who are participating in the choices trading business.

It is hugely a reason for migraines to consider how much benefit you are missing a direct result of the losses happening amid your exchanges. The facts confirm that dangers are always present in all undertakings however a lot of it isn't sound. You may not dispose of them, yet you can, in any case, accomplish something and that is to limit them by utilizing methodologies.

Techniques to be utilized to develop your exchange are resolved as right on time as your arranging stage. These are altogether negligible results of a decent arrangement that is embraced all together for a merchant to seek after his objectives and targets. In the phase of arranging, you will initially consider "what would you like to do?" at that point you will figure "In what manner will you do it?". That is how you will decide the best way to make your exchange fruitful.

Alternatives trading procedures are the determinants of your exchange movement. It will be your instrument in moving which can be contrasted with the steering wheel of a vehicle. These procedures will enable you to decide whether your alternative will run on a flat plane, vertically or corner to corner. However, the inquiry is the best.

When you are allowed to ask every one of the people who is encountering achievement in choices trading on what system they are utilizing, you may get a couple of answers as well as a wide assortment. That is because there is no such thing as a "one size fits all" system in this field. It will be progressively successful if you will redo your very own procedure dependent on your arrangement because as a broker you are the person who splendidly knows every one of the qualities and shortcomings of your exchange so you can decide precisely what will be the best methodology that will be useful for you.

Another significant thing in deciding your system is that you should initially know the basics. Most techniques are only blending of the four primary exchanges, correctly: long call, long put, short call, and shot put. This basic knowledge will be precious in deciding you are a modified viable and effective procedure. You are exceptionally allowed to pick what you think will support you.

As a dealer who needs achievement in the field of choices trading must resemble a chess player. Choices trading, similar to chess, is a clash of systems; the individuals who will have the beyond any doubt win are the individuals who are having their best choices trading procedures. You should remember that your every move will have a significant effect in the entire fight; all things considered; you should turn out to be attentive in your every step. Ensure that you will do is dependable for the success and won't be the purpose behind you to misfortune.

OPTION TRADING STRATEGIES: YOUR GUIDE TO RELIABLE INVESTING

If you are hunting down some elective option trading strategies to help you in your investment ventures? Do you wish to viably deal with your funds and before long make your money work for you? If honestly, read on and perceive how some valuable and down to earth trading strategies and other investment methods can enable you to out.

BRIEF OVERVIEW ON STOCK OPTION TRADING

An investment opportunity is subordinate security because the estimation of the option is "determined" from the opinion of the underlying stock. Mostly, there are two option types: Call options will be options to buy the necessary resource while Put options will be options to sell a hidden resource. On that note, recorded option contracts are institutionalized to encourage trading and value announcing. Such registered investment opportunities give the option holder the privilege to buy or sell 100 offers of stock.

The facts confirm that for some individual traders, joining option trading strategies can have astounding favorable position and potential with negligible hazard if and just if you have comprehended its ideas and standards only as every one of those subtleties and information that might be related with options trade. With that, let us investigate a portion of the key advantages, the upside and the downside of the said trading strategies.

Influence and Influence. When you utilize such strategies on trading options, it permits you to have the chance to take part in some excellent arrangements without having unnecessary assets from inside the more fabulous portfolio.

FLEXIBILITY

For the most part, there are numerous areas in a few option trading strategies which might be connected and utilized for practically any market condition or fair-mindedness position. From its fundamental options trade methodology to elaborate trade set-ups, individual or sole financial specialists can make do with options for a wide range of reasons and goals. Indeed, you are the one to choose as to you intend to go for the fence, holding single option on a stock and the stock itself; to do spread, taking a situation in (at least two) options of a similar kind; and to have the mixing technique, taking a position in the two calls and puts on the same stock. The choice depends on your grasp along with your investment portfolio and vehicle.

Multifaceted nature: For the individual speculator, option trading strategies may be one way or another too much mind-boggling and may in this way be not deserving of your time, exertion, and assets. Since it might appear to be intricate, it is a need that the financial specialists and the prospects experience intensive research, learning, and preparing to have the option to do it right - viably and productively. In any case, amateur and fledglings ought not to stress a lot as there might be available assets over the web that may likewise be solid, objective, and propelled; in this manner, you better search for those with precise setup and vertical dimension considering.

With that, you would now be able to create your investment portfolio and kick off your investment vehicle at its very own advantages and dangers. Begin today by learning and reading more on some reasonable option trade strategies, and obviously, by giving it a significant attempt. Quit agonizing over your accounts and make your well-deserved money work for you at your own pace. Good karma and see you in here once more.

FINDING A SUITABLE PLATFORM FOR YOUR OPTION TRADING STRATEGIES

As online systems and computer information exchange speeds have improved all through the most recent ten years, traders working with option trading strategies have nearly all-around used web stock contributing projects. These online interfaces are getting the opportunity to be very pervasive for the individual speculator. A significant number of us likely can recall the times of really making a call to a dealer to create positions. Anyway, this appears as though it were decades back with current movements.

With the snap of the computer mouse, you can put in buy and sell requests directly through your contributing programming of decision and have demands finished instantly. In any case, while picking a contributing project, you'll be looked at with a variety of options. A lot of prospects and options trading stages "practice" specifically quadrants in the market, for example, foreign currency trading or options trading strategy.

Here are a couple of elements to think about while picking a contributing web project for your options trading strategy:

EXPENSES AND COMMISSION RATES

This goes unwritten, however, the littler the charges and commissions required by the contributing administrations you have picked, the better pay you can clutch. You should distinguish the majority of the administrative expenses associated with the trading account before setting it up for instance request or transaction charges (the fee for each application put), trading account routine upkeep costs, least record adjusts required, and edge charges if you are thinking about trading edges (credited speculation capital) on your trading account. Moreover, many web brokerages charge additional transaction charges for events that you need expert support with a request. Make sure you find out this well before initiating a trading account as some of these trades can be very expensive.

TYPES OF SPECULATIONS ADVERTISED

Again, numerous online stock trading programs offer one kind of venture, however not all. In case you're keen on options trading strategy mainly, you'll be sure to choose an electronic brokerage that offers this administration.

UI

Pretty much every online brokerage firm supplies a particular stock trading stage. Test exhibitions of the contributions that you're thinking about. You'll commit extensive time using the specific graphical UI and features that your favored brokerage offers, and you have to verify that it's easy to understand and well-structured, enabling you moment access to trade execution modules and marketplace information.

PREPARING ASSETS

Nearly all online brokers present you with a wealth of material that is packaged in your administrations. This incorporates learner reports, for instance, data and actualities on essential options trading strategy, and propelled investigation of the marketplace and monetary issues.

SUPPORT ADMINISTRATIONS AND SPECIALIZED SUPPORT

These subjects ought to nearly be unmistakable, yet don't be hesitant to put a couple of email messages or even telephone calls to conceivable web brokerages preceding joining to determine the level of administration which they give to clients. You will require snappy access for mechanical and trading issues amid the normal trading hours. Solicitation or endeavor to build up a contact inside the business and endeavor to gain access to a next phone number or email address in this time for testing. This may come invaluable in case you're ever in a scrape.

VERSATILITY

This has just decently as of late advanced as a factor while picking a web brokerage firm concerning your options trading strategy, yet cell organize speeds have improved amid the most recent three years and mobile phones have developed to feature better quality information preparing ability. In case you contribute with your versatile or convenient gadget, you'll need to determine whether or not your potential online brokerage gives a down to earth contributing stage to your device.

Even though you will discover several decisions for online trading systems on which to do your options trading strategy, with far-reaching due industriousness, you can without a doubt locate the right accomplice for your contributions. Try not to rush through the procedure, and you'll make sure to find a trading accomplice that will be ideal for obliging your options trading strategy and accomplishing your account goals.

Chapter 3

PICKING A STRATEGY BASED ON CURRENT MARKET CONDITIONS

f you have ever worked with an investment before, you know that there are times when the market goes up, when it goes down, and when it stays steady. Each of these conditions will make a difference based on the type of trade that you are working with. The good news is that there are strategies that will work no matter which market condition you want to enter into during your trade. There is always the possibility of making a profit if you do it all the right way.

As someone new to the whole options trading market, you will find that there are a ton of strategies that you can use. But sometimes it is hard to keep all the information straight when you are starting. Here we will take a look at some of the different market scenarios that you can work with at different times in your journey as well as the strategies that you can use to help you make a profit.

THE PRICES RISE JUST A LITTLE

The first market scenario that we will look at is what happens when the price of your security rises a little bit. There are some strategies that you can work with to make this profitable including the bull call spread, the bull put spread and the short put. First, let's take a look at how the bull call spread will work. The benefit of choosing to go with this strategy is that it is more cost-effective in terms of how much you will pay upfront. However, this strategy will not help you make as much profit as some of the others.

Some investors will work with the bull put spread in this market condition. This one is similar to the last one, but you will write the puts on the asset while also purchasing the same number of puts. The good news about this one is that you can earn a profit, regardless of whether your asset rises during this time. However, if the asset ends up earning a huge increase in price, the profits you earn will be limited as well.

And finally, you can work with the short-put strategy. This will ask you to sell an open order where you can write the puts on the asset that you believe will go up in price. The best thing that you can do when working with this one is to write close to the money put options that have a near expiry date. When working with this strategy, you will be able to use a simple strategy. However, if the asset price goes down a lot, then you will lose out on money in the process.

THE PRICES FALL JUST A LITTLE

Some investors choose to work with the bear call spread. When working with the bear call spread, you will write out your calls and then go out and purchase calls that have the same asset and the same expiry, but the ones that you choose to purchase will end up with a high strike price. This one can be confusing to beginners, so it is a strategy that is reserved for traders who are in the market for a long time. You can make a profit with this one, even if the price of the asset doesn't move at all.

And you can also choose to work with the short call. This short call will ask you to write out all of your call options using exactly or near the money, and you will use an order that is known as sell to open. The best way for this one to work is for the options to expire shortly. When you are working with this one, even if the asset barely moves, you will make a good profit. If the asset price goes down a lot, you can lose out on money.

THE PRICES RAISES A LOT

There are times when the market will see some dramatic shifts in how well it is doing. If you are looking at an asset and you believe that it will see a dramatic increase in its price soon, there are a couple of strategies that you may want to go with including the long call and the short bull ratio.

The long call is the first one that you may want to consider in this scenario. With this one, you will buy an open order to purchase calls. The biggest advantage of using the long call is that if you see the price go up by a lot on that asset, you will be able to make limitless profits. However, if you see that the security doesn't change in price or if the price goes down within the expiry date, then you will have no protection against a loss.

Another option that you can work with if the price of the asset will go up by a large amount is the bull ratio spread. This is another one that is often saved for those who have been in the market for a long time. With this particular strategy, you will buy and write calls for the same asset, and these both need to expire at the same time. You must make sure that you are purchasing more options than you are writing. The biggest reason to go with this one is that you will still have protection for yourself if there is a fall in the asset price, or if that price doesn't move at all, you will still be able to earn something, but the potential profit is not as high as some other options.

THE PRICES FALL A LOT

There will be times when the market will go down quite a bit. If you look at an asset and there are signs that this asset will see a decrease in value shortly, it is time to work with either the short bear ratio spread or the long put. The long put is a simple strategy to work with and can be a good one to work with if you are a beginner. To work with this one, you must make sure that your broker and you can buy to open order and then buy a put option on that same asset. It is always best when working with this option that you purchase at the money contracts.

What this means is that the strike price should be the same as the market price. Doing this will ensure that you have a handle on your risk for each trade. If you ever feel that an asset will fall soon, you can go with a contract that has a close expiration date. The disadvantage of working with this strategy is that if the asset price doesn't rise or it doesn't move at all, you will have no way to cut your losses and leave early.

The other strategy that you can work with in this market scenario is the short bear ratio spread. This one is a little harder to work with. You will start with purchasing puts and writing puts at the same time. These all need to be for the same asset with the same expiration date, but the written put must have a higher strike price. You also need to go and purchase more contracts than you will sell. This can be nice because it will provide some protection if the asset price doesn't go the way that you want, but it will not add as much profit to your pockets as other strategies.

THE PRICES RISE TO A CERTAIN NUMBER

If you are looking at an asset and you feel that it will reach a specific number and that it will get to this point within a certain amount of time, then there are a few different strategies that you can work with. Some of the best strategies for doing this include the bull butterfly spread and the bull condor spread. When you are working with the bull butterfly spread, you will work with three transactions, so it is something reserved for those who have more experience in the market.

For every two calls that you decide to write, you will need to purchase one call that is at the next highest strike price. This option is a good one to go with because it will provide you with a ton of profits. However, you will not have a limit on how much you can use when working with this strategy.

If you want to get even more complex, you can use the bull condor spread that has four transactions. With this one, you will write calls with each strike price on the lower end of the price range that you want the asset to rise to, while also writing a few calls on the higher end. You can also buy calls at the higher and the lower strike price. The strategy can be great for profits, but since there are so many transactions in the process, remember that you will have to pay your broker more to complete this.

SECURITY FALLS TO A SPECIFIC NUMBER

For this one, you believe that the asset you will invest in will fall to a specific number. The best choice to do with this one is the bear butterfly spread, but there are three transactions that have to occur for this one. You will write the put options at whatever price you think the asset will fall to, and then for every two puts that you end up writing, you are also going to purchase two put options. One of these needs to be a higher strike price and the other should be lower with them both expiring at the same time. The advantage of doing this one is that you won't end up losing as much money if the asset doesn't move at price the way that you would like. However, commissions can add up because you are ordering three different transactions.

THE PRICE CAN GO UP OR DOWN

There will be times when the market will have a lot of ups and downs and will be very volatile. This can make it hard to figure out whether the price of the asset will go up or down during your investment time. You may be certain that there will be a big movement in some direction, but you are not sure which direction it will go. There are still a few strategies that you can use to make this work as well including the long straddle, long strangle, long gut, and short butterfly spread.

The first one that we will look at is the long straddle. This can be a good strategy because it will help you to increase how much potential profit you can make. But if you end up not having a big change in the asset you choose, then you will end up losing money. The long strangle can work similarly, but it is much cheaper than working with the other option, but you will need to see as big of a price change in your asset to make a profit.

It is also possible to work with the long gut. This is a great strategy to work with as a beginner because it will involve buying in the money call options and then also purchasing in the money put options at the same time. All the things that you will purchase will have the same expiration date and, in the end, you will have the same amount of call and put options. If you feel that the asset will move soon, then you should make sure that the options you purchase have a short expiration date.

If you have spent some time working in options trading, then you may want to try with the short butterfly spread. There will end up being three transactions for this one, including selling in the money calls, buying twice as many at the money calls, and selling the same amount of out of the money calls. All of the options that you work with will end up with an expiration date that is the same. For the strike prices that you will work with, your out of the money calls should be proportional to the in the money calls that you work with. If you have a strike price that is close to the asset price, then you will not need to see a ton of movement to make a profit, but the amount you make will be a lot lower.

NO CHANGE IN PROFITS

The final thing that you will want to watch out for in the market is when you do not think the asset will move at all during your trading time. There are a few strategies that will work well with this option such as the short straddle, short strangle, and the butterfly spread.

To start, you will want to try out the short straddle. This is considered a higher level of trading because it will ask the trader to sell to open order so that you can write at the money calls. Also, you must do the same number of puts on the same asset to make this work. Both the puts and the calls need to have the same expiration date to work.

You can also choose to work with the short strangle. To do the short strangle, you must write call options that are equal to how many puts that you write. These all need to be out of the money calls. If you go with a contract that is considered out of the money, the price of the asset that you go with will need to see a really large movement before you will lose any money. However, if you choose to go with an expiration that is shorter in terms of your options, then you will be more likely to get a profit out of this.

You can also work with the butterfly spread to help you out in this kind of market condition, although this is not a strategy that most beginners will go with. This is because the butterfly spread will be difficult to work with and it becomes more expensive than some of the other options. It can be attractive in the beginning because it has a lower upfront cost, but there are a lot of transactions that you need to do to make the butterfly spread work and when you do all those different transactions, those commissions that you pay will start to add up quickly.

As you can see, there are a lot of different conditions that you can find in the market, but there are strategies that can work with each one. You will be able to pick out a good strategy, no matter which market condition you are working with, and still end up with a profit in the end. Make sure to learn how to work with at least a few different strategies so that you can make as much money on options as possible.

Chapter 4
IRON CONDOR STRATEGY

I f you think the price of a stock will stay within a certain range, you can sell to open an iron condor. This type of strategy requires you to buy a call and sell a call (creating a call credit spread) and buy a put and sell a put (creating a put credit spread). Let's see how it is built-in steps. All options in this strategy have the same expiration date.

First, you pick an out of the money call price, a bit above the current share price. You sell this call. Then you buy one with a strike that is a little bit higher. The net difference gives you a credit.

Now you pick an out of the money put option, that is below the current share price. Then you sell this put option. Next, you buy an out of the money put option that has an even lower strike price. The difference here gives you another credit.

The maximum profit is the net credits. The maximum loss is given by (width of strike prices) − entry price. The broker will make you put up enough cash to cover the loss unless you have a margin account.

The narrower you make your strike prices the lower your maximum loss, but the higher the probability that you will experience a loss. The range is set by the two options you sell, you want the stock price to stay within those bounds.

The iron condor is a great strategy to use for monthly income. It can work especially well over short time frames, like a week, since that lessens the chance of the stock going outside the range. However, many traders use a month for their iron condors.

This strategy combines the bear call spread, and the bull put spread. It involves selling an out-of-the-money put and purchasing an out-of-the-money put at a lower strike price. You then sell an out-of-the-money call to buy a call at higher strike prices. All these options are initiated at the same expiration date and on the same stock value.

The iron condor strategy is mostly applied to low volatile stocks to earn a net premium from the options spread. The combination of put and call options makes this strategy non-directional, thus creating a possibility to make profits either on the upside or downside. You can apply it to short-term or long-term trades depending on the performance of the market. The higher the trading range, the higher the profits realized.

Most beginners are always eager to start trading that they forget to look for the appropriate knowledge and skills for success. These strategies allow you to maximize profits on your options trading account. You must take time and build a solid foundation that will increase your chances of succeeding in your trades. The idea is if you do not know what you are doing, you will end up losing your money. With a good strategy, you can start making profits as soon as you start trading.

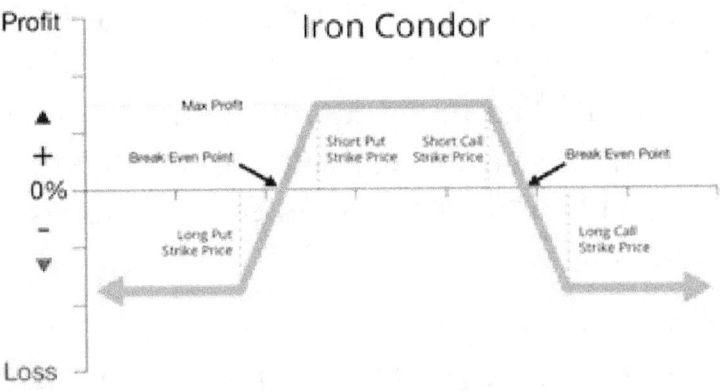

Iron Condor

Out of all the strategies that we will discuss in this guidebook, this one has the highest potential to give you profits and it has the least amount of risk as well.

You will use the iron condor to trade on stocks with very low volatility. It is not a good idea to go with a stock that moves around quite a bit and has big highs and lows that go all over the place. You will find that this is a credit spread strategy that will be viewed as a combination of the bear call spread (which we talk about in the following chapter) and the bull put spread.

You can consider the iron condor as a type of evergreen strategy, one that a lot of traders will use when they find a stable stock. As a trader, if you can choose any strategy and you want to go with one that is pretty easy to follow and will give you a higher probability of doing well, then the iron condor is the best option for you to choose.

The iron condor will be a little bit more difficult to work with because there are four legs to go with it, rather than the two legs on the other trading strategy. For the first step, you need to go through and find the stock that you would like to work with. Remember that for the iron condor to work, you need to have a stock that is pretty stable and won't go up or down too much in the process.

The next step is to sell one deep OOTM put option of the stock that you selected. Then buy one OOTM put option with the same expiry date and with the same stock that you sold in the first step, but make sure that this one has a lower strike price.

After those steps are done, it is time to sell again. This time you will sell a deep OOTM but it needs to be a call option. You want this to use the same stock and have the same expiry date as what you used in the last part. And finally, you can buy an OOTM call option that has the same stock and the same expiry date as all the other steps, but this one needs to have a slightly higher strike-price.

One thing to note is that there will be a difference between the strike prices the two put options need to be the same as the difference between the strikes of the two call options if you want to accurately create this strategy. Throughout the time until the expiry, you will want to monitor how your position is doing. Unless you are certain that your stock will keep within the limits that you have placed, you will want to consider exiting out of the trade when the position is making 50% or more of the maximum profit that you want out of this trade. If you find that the market goes against your expectations and there is a big directional movement of your stock, it is time to close out all of the positions and wait until that stock has time to stabilize before entering again.

You would choose to go with this strategy any time that your stock is showing a really low amount of volatility. This means that the stock is not moving much or if it is moving within a range that you can define easily. For the most part, index options are the best for executing this strategy compared to stock-based options since these indexes are often less volatile. If you are working with a pretty stable market, you will find that iron condors are the safest option for winning.

The biggest advantage of using the iron condor is that it is considered a neutral position and you are likely to get some kind of profit as long as you execute this strategy the right way, no matter which way your chosen stock or index ends up moving. And since this is a net credit strategy, it will be able to help you work against the issues with time decay.

The biggest disadvantage that you will find with the iron condor is that the returns that you will get out of it are quite a bit less than what you can get from a directional strategy. Also, the maximum loss that you can incur will be quite a bit more than the maximum profit that you would be able to gain in this position if you are not careful with the stocks that you are using. However, when looking at the statistics for success with the iron condor, you will notice that the probability of a win will be much higher than that of a loss, which helps to make this a great strategy to work with.

You will use the iron condor to trade on stocks with very low volatility. It is not a good idea to go with a stock that moves around quite a bit and has big highs and lows that go all over the place. You will find that this is a credit spread strategy that will be viewed as a combination of the bear call spread (which we talk about in the following chapter) and the bull put spread.

You can consider the iron condor as a type of evergreen strategy, one that a lot of traders will use when they find a stable stock. As a trader, if you can choose any strategy and you want to go with one that is pretty easy to follow and will give you a higher probability of doing well, then the iron condor is the best option for you to choose.

The iron condor will be a little bit more difficult to work with because there are four legs to go with it, rather than the two legs on the other trading strategy. For the first step, you need to go through and find the stock that you would like to work with. Remember that for the iron condor to work, you need to have a stock that is pretty stable and won't go up or down too much in the process.

The next step is to sell one deep OOTM put option of the stock that you selected. Then buy one OOTM put option with the same expiry date and with the same stock that you sold in the first step, but make sure that this one has a lower strike price.

After those steps are done, it is time to sell again. This time you will sell a deep OOTM but it needs to be a call option. You want this to use the same stock and have the same expiry date as what you used in the last part. And finally, you can buy an OOTM call option that has the same stock and the same expiry date as all the other steps, but this one needs to have a slightly higher strike-price.

One thing to note is that there will be a difference between the strike prices the two put options need to be the same as the difference between the strikes of the two call options if you want to accurately create this strategy. Throughout the time until the expiry, you will want to monitor how your position is doing. Unless you are certain that your stock will keep within the limits that you have placed, you will want to consider exiting out of the trade when the position is making 50% or more of the maximum profit that you want out of this trade. If you find that the market goes against your expectations and there is a big directional movement of your stock, it is time to close out all of the positions and wait until that stock has time to stabilize before entering again.

You would choose to go with this strategy any time that your stock is showing a really low amount of volatility. This means that the stock is not moving much or if it is moving within a range that you can define easily. For the most part, index options are the best for executing this strategy compared to stock-based options since these indexes are often less volatile. If you are working with a pretty stable market, you will find that iron condors are the safest option for winning.

The biggest advantage of using the iron condor is that it is considered a neutral position and you are likely to get some kind of profit as long as you execute this strategy the right way, no matter which way your chosen stock or index ends up moving. And since this is a net credit strategy, it will be able to help you work against the issues with time decay.

The biggest disadvantage that you will find with the iron condor is that the returns that you will get out of it are quite a bit less than what you can get from a directional strategy. Also, the maximum loss that you can incur will be quite a bit more than the maximum profit that you would be able to gain in this position if you are not careful with the stocks that you are using. However, when looking at the statistics for success with the iron condor, you will notice that the probability of a win will be much higher than that of a loss, which helps to make this a great strategy to work with.

For this one, the trader can hold onto the short and the long position at the same time, but you need to make sure that there are two strangles that are separate. This is a good one to go with to help you get started with selling the options because it is impossible to experience a loss on both sides with this trade. What this means for you as the trader is that you are only going to end up losing on one side, but you can end up with a win, or a profit, on the other side. So, you will end up winning one way or another when you use the iron condor method.

Chapter 5
THE BEAR CALL SPREAD STRATEGY

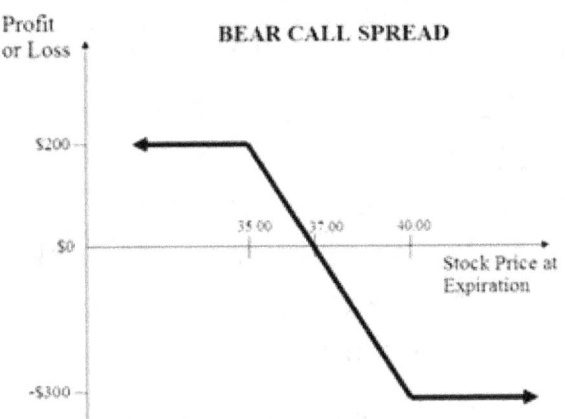

Next on the list is the bear call spread. This is another directional strategy that will be used by a trader when they believe that their underlying stock has reached its upper resistance level and they do not believe that the underlying stock will go up much more at this point. They usually believe that the price point of the stock will stay flat and not change or it will go back down. This will be the opposite strategy that we talked about earlier with the bull put spread.

Like the bull put spread, the bear call spread is also a credit spread. What this means is the premium that you end up receiving while selling one leg of this trade will be greater than any premium that you end up paying for the second leg of the trade. You will end up receiving a net credit to your account when you decide to go with this position.

The first step in creating your bear call spread is to select the right stock that fits this kind of strategy. You will find that there are a variety of stocks that you can choose from, but you will need to pick based on your outlook for this kind of index.

Next, you will need to sell an OOTM call option of the stock that you selected. And third, you should purchase an OOTM call option that has the same expiry date and the same underlying stock as your id with your ATM call option, but the second one needs to have a higher strike price.

Once you enter the market, you will want to constantly monitor your position each day. Once you have made a considerable profit, which is about 50% of your max profit, it is time to exit your position. Or, once you have started to recognize some of the signs of the market and you are sure that the stock won't end up reversing, you could wait until the stock reaches its expiry and then take the maximum amount of profit.

Sometimes spans are crowned as better for entering a bear call spread than others. You would want to choose the bear call spread any time that you believe that your chosen stock is not likely to rise in price shortly and that this stock is probably going to decline from its current price rather than go up. This can happen when the stock from a particular company that had big market expectations posted their results and these were way below the expectations of the market. Also, the index option could hit a big resistance level, and this could cause it to go down a bit.

This method won't work that well if the stock is volatile and it has the potential to rise quite a bit over the short term. You want to pick out some options that are not likely to go up anymore. You would then be able to use the bear call spread and make some profit whether the stock stays stagnant or the price goes down.

The maximum profit that you will be able to make with the bear call spread is when at the time of expiry, the stock price is trading below the strike price of the call option that was sold. To get the maximum profit, you will need to take the premium received or sell the lower-strike call option and minus the premium paid for purchasing the higher-strike call option. Then you can multiply both of these by the lot size.

The biggest loss that you would incur with this kind of spread is when at the time of expiry, the stock price is trading above the strike price call option you bought with the higher strike price. This is why you want to make sure that you are picking out stocks that will go down or remain steady. If the stock goes up with this option, you will end up losing money in the process.

This is why this strategy is a good one to choose if you think that the market is about to go down or you want to work with a stock that is not increasing at the time.

The biggest advantage of working with the bear call spread is that it will ensure that the time-decay will work in your favor. As long as you go with a stock that can stay below your lower strike-price when the expiry happens, you will get the benefit of keeping your entire credit that you received when you entered into this position and you have the potential to make a good profit.

However, there is a disadvantage of working with this strategy. With this position, if you see that there is the possibility that the stock will make a big movement that goes against your expectations. This means that the stock starts rising in price quickly rather than remaining stagnant or going down as you had predicted. If this does happen, the maximum amount that you could lose can be a lot more than the maximum profit that you might have been able to gain with this strategy so there is some risk.

Chapter 6
MARRIED PUT STRATEGY

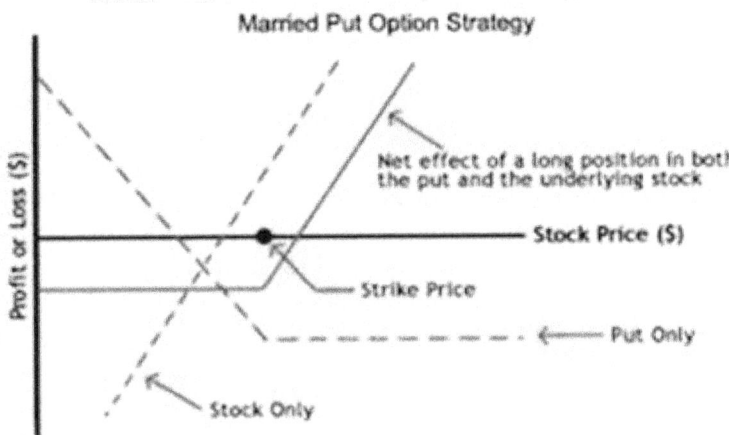

Married Put Option Strategy

Net effect of a long position in both the put and the underlying stock

Stock Price ($)

Strike Price

Put Only

Stock Only

Profit or Loss ($)

I n this strategy, you purchase or you currently own a given asset like shares, and at the same time, you purchase a put option for an equal number of shares. You can use this strategy if you think the price of an asset will go up in the near term and if you wish to protect yourself against short-term losses. This strategy generally functions like insurance policies and therefore establishes a floor if the price of the asset was to plunge dramatically.

It will be a combination of the two strategies that we talked about above, and it can be a good way to make some profit while also protecting yourself. With this strategy, you will purchase the asset that you wish to use while at the same time doing a put option for them. This is a good choice for some investors because it will protect you against short-term losses that can occur inside the market.

Chapter 7
PROTECTIVE COLLAR STRATEGY

Protective Collar Options Strategy

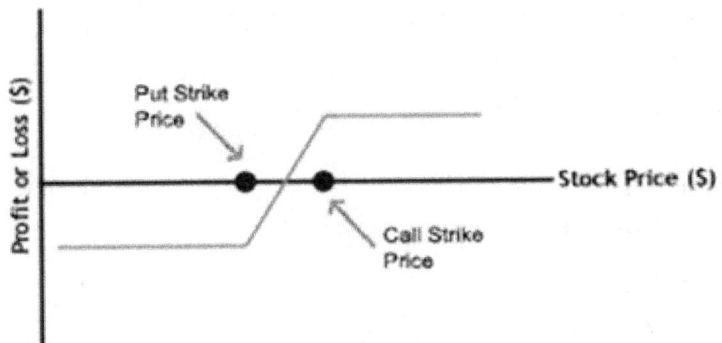

A nother strategy that you can choose to go with as a beginner is known as the protective collar. For this one, you would want to purchase an out of the money put option. At the same time, you will also write an out of the money call option. This is the strategy that a trader will use when they see that the long position they went with is still doing well. The protective collar will then let the trader lock in those profits without needing to go out and sell the shares they own in the process.

This strategy is done by purchasing an OOTM put option and simultaneously writing an OOTM call option for the same underlying asset. You can use this strategy after a long position in a given stock has accumulated substantial gains. This way, you can lock a profit without having to sell your shares.

The protective collar strategy comprises an out-of-the-money put option and a call option that run concurrently. This strategy is not so common in beginners, but if you master it correctly, you can lock some good profits from it. The combination of call and put options allows you to have downside protection to your stock while enjoying potential profits on the upside. It is the same as running the covered call and protective put strategies at the same time.

Investors use this strategy as another option to stop orders since they have the right to choose when to exercise their options. You can implement this strategy with little or no cost since the premium you get from the short call can be used to cancel out the cost of the long put. The strategy is called a collar because it helps you limit both downside and upside risk.

Chapter 8
LONG STRADDLE STRATEGY

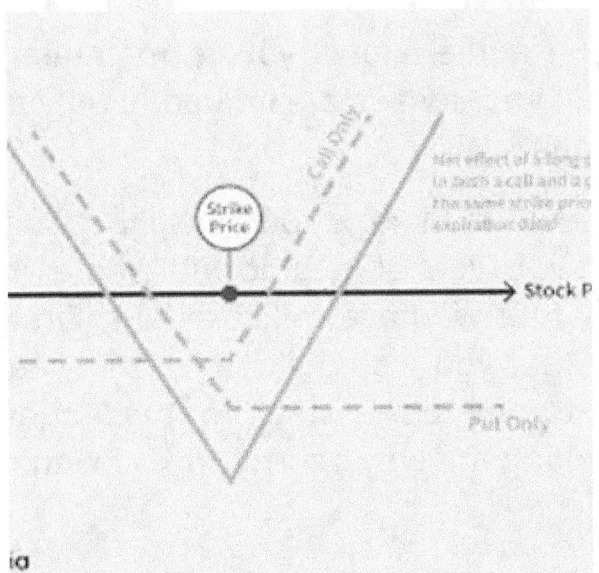

This strategy is one where you will need to go and pick out an option that you want to work with. When you find the right asset, you will buy a put and a call on this asset. Both of these orders will work with the same strike price and expiration date. This is a good strategy to go with when you know that the price of the asset will have some dramatic moves shortly, but you may not know which way (either up or down) that the asset will move. This will ensure that you can make some money regardless of which way the trade ends up going.

You can use this strategy when you simultaneously purchase a put and call option that has a similar underlying asset, strike price, and expiration date. Most traders use this strategy when they believe the price of an underlying asset will have a significant movement but are unsure in which direction the move will be.

The long straddle allows you to maintain unlimited gains while your losses are limited to only the cost of both options.

So, to execute the long straddle will be a bit different than what you were able to do with some of the other strategies that we have talked about. First, pick out the stock that you would like to do. To see success, you need to pick out a stock that will show a lot of volatility along the way shortly, or you won't get good results.

After you have chosen the stock that you want to work with, you need to purchase an ATM call option of this stock. Then you need to purchase an ATM put option that has the same stock and the same expiry date as the call option that you purchased in the previous step.

When you complete the purchases, you will want to watch your trade pretty closely. When you see the large price movement that you were watching out for, it is time to close the legs at the same time. This is another strategy that will have to fight against the time decay issue and this time decay will impact both options, so it is best to not hold onto this kind of strategy for over a few days.

One thing to note is that the strike prices of both your put and your call options need to be the same when doing the straddle trade. This can be difficult to do when entering into a trade though and you may not be able to purchase the options when the market price of the stock isn't matching up to your chosen strike price. When doing this trade, you may find that the market price of your chosen stock might end up being slightly above or below the chosen strike price of your option. This implies that you have a likelihood of ending up with one option that is slightly OOTM and the other one ends up being slightly ITM when you initiate this kind of trade. This is fine as long as you keep them as close to the ATM as possible.

The long straddle and strangle is a strategy that you are only supposed to use on rare occasions and only when you think that there will be a sudden and big rise or fall in the stock you want to choose, usually following some external factor. Even in this kind of trade, when you enter into the long straddle position, you want to make sure that the volatility still isn't too high. Most traders will stick with a stock or an index that is less than 60%of historical volatility.

The reason that you want to be careful with this is that if there is a big drop in the volatility of the stock, even after the price movement goes the way that you want, this drop-in volatility will end up harming how much profit you can make.

- The quarterly or annual results from a company will come out in the next few days and people have some big expectations from these.

- A big decision regarding the company that owns the stocks will come out soon. This could include a decision for the company to change their management or to do a merger with another company.

- A big announcement that will talk about a large dividend or a bonus issue will come out soon.

If you are working with a benchmark index, many situations could make it rise or fall. Some of these would include the announcements of the annual budget for the company, when the company will make some new monetary policy decisions when there are some major elections in the management of the company, and even some major socio-economic decisions. If you see that any of these will happen with the underlying stock, it may be time to work with this position.

On the other hand, if you see that your chosen stock is trading on a pretty narrow range, or if you feel that the outlook on that stock is pretty neutral (without much movement even if it is negative or positive) over the short-term, then the long straddle strategy is not the right one for you. It should also be a strategy that you avoid if the volatility is high, even if there is some potential for movement.

The primary advantage that you will see when working with the long straddle is that you do have the potential to earn unlimited profits as soon as the trade crosses the break-even point, no matter what direction it goes in. The straddle is often used to earn profits even when a stock is volatile in the market without having to worry about predicting which direction that the stock will move in and for how long. Volatile stocks often go up and down pretty quickly and it is hard to figure out which way you should go. With this strategy, you will have the opportunity to profit from a rise and a fall of your stock based on the points that you pick.

Another benefit that you can find with the straddle position is that it will limit how much risk you are exposed to. The amount of risk that you will face is the total amount of premium that you paid when you decided to enter into the trade with this stock.

The biggest disadvantage that comes with using the long straddle is that you will have to deal with the time decay issue. The time decay issue could affect both sides of your straddle trade, the call, and the put, so this issue is compounded and can cause you more issues than you would have with other strategies.

Another disadvantage of using this kind of position to earn a profit is that it can be a bit difficult. To earn a profit, you need to properly predict that your chosen stock will have a very sharp movement, either up or down, in a pretty short amount of time.

Chapter 9
LONG STRANGLE STRATEGY

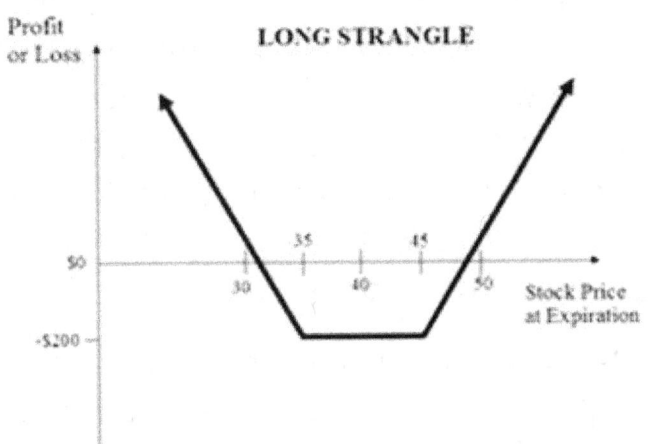

his one will feel a lot like the long straddle, but there will be a few differences that help it to be all its own. One of the major differences that you will see is that while the put and the pull options are still the same and will be on the same asset and expiration date, they will come in with a different strike price for both of these. The price that you will use on your call options will be a bit higher compared to the price that you put on the put strike. However, both of these prices are out of the money. This option is less expensive than working with the long straddle, but it will be a choice to go with when you think that the asset price will go up or down quite a bit shorter.

In this strategy, you simultaneously purchase a put and call option with the expiration date and underlying asset, but at different strike prices. The strike price of the put option will be lower than the strike price of the call option. Both options should also be out of the money.

Use this strategy when you believe the price of an underlying asset will have a large movement, but you are unsure in which direction the move shall be. The losses you incur with this strategy are limited to the cost of the two options. A long strangle is typically cheaper than straddles because the options are purchased out of the money.

The advantage of going with this long strangle rather than the long straddle is that the amount of premium that you will have to pay for your premiums will be less than what you have to pay with the long straddle. However, for the long strangle to work, you will need the move in the market to be much bigger to recover your costs.

Traders will profit using the long strangle any time that they see a sharp move in their stock, similar to using the long straddle position, and you still have the potential to make unlimited profits. However, with this strategy, the maximum loss will happen if the price of the stock settles between the strike price for the call and the put when you reach the time of expiry. The maximum loss though, in both the straddle and the strangle, will be the premiums that you paid for the put and the call options.

Chapter 10
THE IRON BUTTERFLY STRATEGY

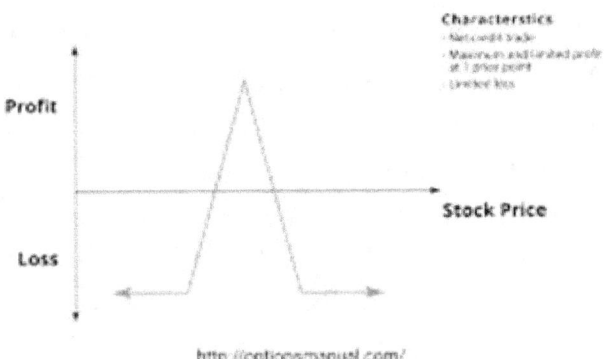

Execute An Iron butterfly

http://optionsmanual.com/

An iron butterfly is another strategy to use if you think the stock price will stay within a certain range. It will use four options, like the iron condor, but there will be three different strike prices.

In this case, you will sell a put option and a call option with the same strike price. The strategy is to get as close to the money as possible. We will call the strike price using the central strike. Then you set a differential price we will call x. Now you buy a put option with a strike price of (central strike − x), and you buy a call option with a strike price of (central strike + x).

Because the strategy allows you to sell two options at the same strike price, it is considered one of the low-price strategies that beginners can take advantage of. However, since it utilizes spreads of long and short calls, the chances of getting large profits are relatively slim. If the strike price is higher than the premium, the trade is considered to be bullish, and if it is lower than the premium, it is a bearish trade.

Like an iron condor, the profit from an iron butterfly is fixed at the net credit when you sell to open. This is given by the sum of the premiums earned from selling them at the money call and put, minus the prices paid for the out of the money options.

The maximum loss is the strike price of the purchased call − strike price of the sold put − total premium.

In this strategy, you combine either a short or a long straddle with a simultaneous sale or purchase of a long strangle. The only difference this strategy has to the butterfly spread is that it uses both puts and calls.

The loss or profit you can gain from this strategy is limited to a specific range depending on the strike prices of the options used. OOTM works best with this strategy to cut down on costs and at the same time, limit your risks.

The trader will be able to limit their risks by using an out of the money option. The trader will be able to combine a short or long straddle with a purchase, or they will be able to do a sale of a strangle at the same time. It is a bit different than other strategies because you will need to work with calls and puts to make it work.

As you can see, there are quite a few different strategies that you can work with depending on how the market is doing and which options you would like to go with. Take a look at some of the different strategies to help you figure out which one is the best for you and will help you to make as much money as possible.

Chapter 11
COVERED CALL STRATEGY

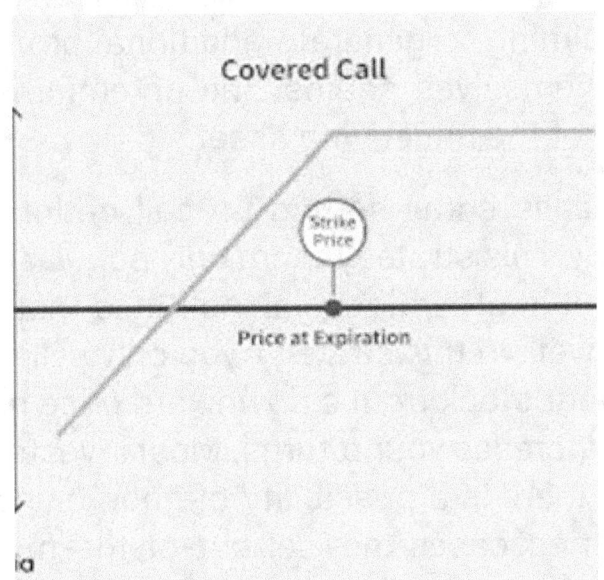

his can be a good strategy to work with when a trader is trying to earn a profit from a call premium while also trying to protect themselves against the possibility of the asset losing value shortly. With this one, if you notice that the volatility in the market increases, the trader has the possibility of losing. However, if the volatility slows down, then the trader could gain.

Besides purchasing a plain call option (naked call option), you can also use the covered call strategy (also referred to as the buy-write strategy). In this strategy, you purchase the assets outright then at the same time, write/sell a call option on the same assets. The volume of assets you own should be equal to the number of underlying assets of the call option.

Investors often use this strategy when they have a neutral opinion and short-term position on the assets and are aiming to generate additional profits or just protect themselves against the potential decline of the value of the underlying asset.

Covered calls entail setting up call options against your stock. This strategy is not only popular in options trading but in other financial institutes that deal with stock as well. In this strategy, you only sell options to protect your stock from a downward price movement and also increase your returns. Most investors do this any time there is a possibility of good gains on their stock. In most cases, they sell out-of-the-money calls, and once the price goes high, they trade the stock for a profit.

One advantage of this strategy is that you get to keep your stock at expiration if it falls below the strike price. If the stock goes above the strike price, you will sell the stock shares to the buyer at the strike price. Most investors use this strategy to generate profit at limited risks while retaining their stock.

The downside of covered calls is that you need at least 100 shares of stock to make the calls. The strategy is thus not beneficial for traders who wish to start small.

Traders are also allowed to sell only one call option against 100 stock shares. This is called a covered call because, if the stock price goes high, the call will be covered by the position of your stock.

You can consider using this strategy to make a profit if you already have the required stock and do not expect its cost to go high soon.

Covered calls is a strategy many investors will use when they start trading options. A covered call takes place when the investor owns a stock and decides to sell a call on that stock; i.e., the sale of the stock is covered by the stock owned by the investor. The main reason people do this is to gain additional earnings, for an out of the money stock. A covered call becomes profitable when it expires worthless, that is, it does not become in the money, ITM. The seller of the options collects the premium and keeps the stock. Another reason is to lock in substantial gains.

Example:

Juan owns several hundred shares of Dow Chemical (DOW) that he bought several years ago at $36. DOW is now selling at about $54 and he would like to lock in that gain. He chooses to sell covered calls for a $5 premium with a strike price of $49. That way, Juan becomes a writer and, unless DOW drops to or below the strike price, he collects $500 for every 100-share option he sells. And, if DOW does drop to that level before expiration, the option protects his gain of $13. (49 - 36 = 13.) per share. Good insurance.

Chapter 12
NAKED CALLS STRATEGY

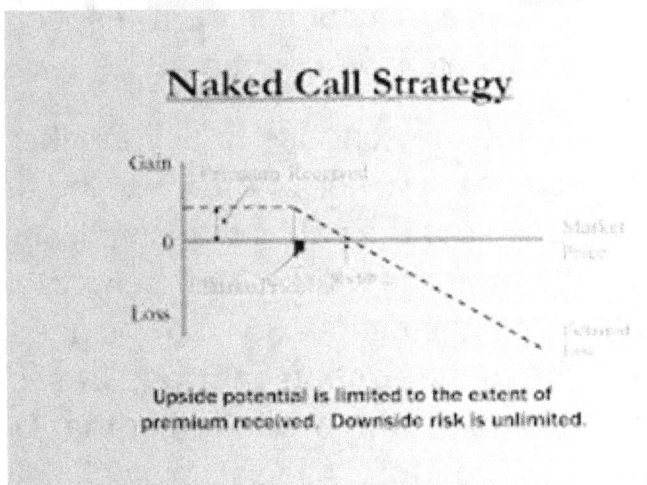

Naked Call Strategy

Gain

0

Loss

Market Price

Upside potential is limited to the extent of
premium received. Downside risk is unlimited.

This is a strategy that you will go with when you are willing to take on a bit more risk, but it is not always a good idea for those who are just beginning to learn the ropes. When you go with this strategy, you will sell a call option on the open market, but you are not the one who owns that asset. If the trade doesn't work out the way that you would like, you may end up losing a lot of money. However, if the trade does work out well for you, it can gain you a good return on investment.

Naked calls occur when an investor sells a call option on a stock she does not own. Naked options are riskier than covered options and can result in almost unlimited losses. But, under the right circumstances, they can be profitable. In effect, you are selling to someone else the right to buy a stock you do not own, and if required, you would have to go into the market and buy the stock at market price. This is a more advanced strategy usually limited by your broker, based on the value of your account, especially the value of the cash held in your account.

For example, Alice may choose to sell a naked call in DOW. She becomes a writer of the call. She does not own Dow shares so if the call is exercised, she would have to buy them at the market and sell at the strike price. DOW is trading at about $54, so she needs to set up an out of the money option contract. Based on her reading of the market, she wants to bet that DOW will decline in price. Therefore, Alice sells a call on DOW at say, 57. That means, if the price drops below the strike price of 57, she keeps the premium and does not have to deliver the stock. If instead, DOW surges up before the expiration date, she will have to deliver the stock. That means she must go into the market and buy DOW at the market price and deliver it. When a stock is very volatile, the potential loss can be essentially unlimited, that is, the loss is limited only by the rise in market price.

Example:

Charlie has been watching Tesla Motor Company, TSLA. TSLA has recently been at about $200 but recent news causes Charlie to think the market may go down substantially. Beta for TSLA is 0.72 which means it tends to lag the market but that does not account for the recent news. Charlie sells or writes a naked call for TSLA with a strike price of $185 with a premium of $10. This means that if TSLA goes down below $185, the option will expire and he keeps the premium of $1000, which is $10 times 100 shares. His profit must be calculated with the commission included, which reduces the profit a little.

Chapter 13

CASH SECURED PUTS STRATEGY

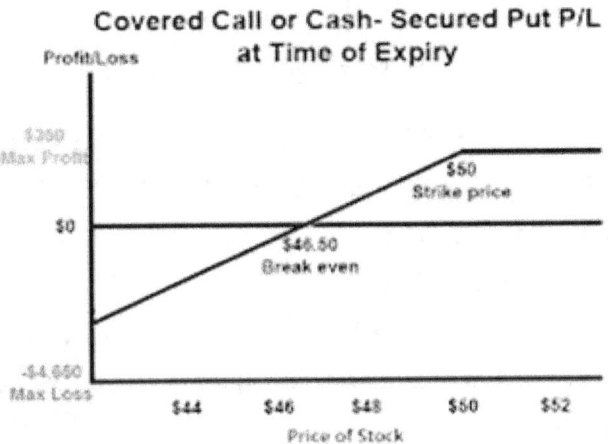

Covered Call or Cash- Secured Put P/L at Time of Expiry

This is the opposite of covered calls. This strategy requires you to sell puts against a liquid cash balance in your broker account. The only people who use this strategy are investors anticipating a decline in the stock price or those traders who wish to generate some profit from excess cash that is in their possession. Through selling puts against their cash, they can make some profit.

Generally, this strategy involves selling put options while saving enough cash on the side to purchase the underlying stock. It allows you to get stock options at discounted prices and sell them at a profit. The goal is to acquire the underlying stock at a price that is below the market price.

When the stock goes below the strike price, the put is assigned, and the trader is allowed to buy the stock at the strike price. The process involves a lot of risks since the stock may decrease way below the strike price and this means that you may be required to purchase the shares at an amount that is above the current stock price. This comes as a loss to you, especially if the prices keep going down.

This is where an investor buys stock and equivalent put options simultaneously. You can sell the put option at the strike price. Just like the covered call, each married put contract requires 100 shares. In this case, the trader is positive that the stock value will rise but uses a put option as insurance should the value go down.

The married put strategy is common in investors who have a vision of minimizing the downside risk of their stock. When an investor buys the shares and an option, he protects his stock from loss should a negative event occur and also makes some cash as the stock's value increases. However, if the stock does not go down, the investor loses the cash placed on the put option as a premium.

The married put has so many similarities with the covered call. It gets its name from combining or marrying a put option with the underlying stock. For every 100 shares, you are only allowed to buy one put option.

The maximum profit for this strategy is undefined. The more the stock appreciates, the higher the profits. One downside of this strategy lies in the cost of premiums. The put option increases in value as the stock value declines, and because of this, the trader loses the cost placed on the option. Such losses, however, cannot be compared to the value of the underlying stock which would have been saved in the process.

Chapter 14
BEAR PUT SPREAD STRATEGY

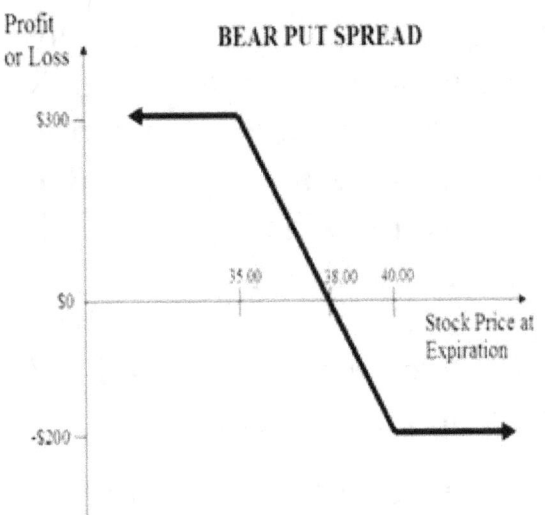

This is one of the best strategies for beginners since it involves short put spreads. The bear put spread can easily be applied to small and new trading accounts. It does not have any restrictions in terms of shares or premiums. It is also known as the short put spread and involves the selling of puts.

You can use this strategy when expecting the stock to remain at the same value or increase in price until the expiration date. If this happens, the option will expire worthlessly, and you will get your whole premium back.

To set up the bear put spread, start by selling a put option, then purchase another put option with a lower strike price than the one you sold. The option you buy should have the same value and expiration date as the one you sold. This makes your sold out more expensive than the one you bought, translating into some profit.

Unlike the long call, which returns multiple times of the investment, the short put spread can only give you a maximum return that is equal to your initial premium. This amount will be determined by the direction of the market. If the stock remains at the same level or goes beyond the strike price, you will get your premium back. If the stock decreases below the strike price, you will be forced to purchase the underlying stock at the strike price, and this results in a loss.

Investors use this vertical spread strategy to make a profit from selling premiums to other investors who have bet against the stock prices going up. Because put sellers often have a certain number of shares to their name, they cannot get stuck when it comes to paying out on losses. In case you need to use this strategy, you must be careful that you do not sell your puts without first understanding the market. This is because stock prices may fall and claim all your premiums.

This is another directional strategy that you will want to employ any time that you have a negative outlook on your chosen stock. This means that you are taking a look at a stock and you expect that shortly, it will fall moderately. This is another debit spread, just like the bull call spread that we discussed earlier, which means that you will be in charge of paying a debt to enter into the position.

To get started with this kind of strategy, you will want to pick out the right stock that will fit into the criteria that are needed for this strategy. Remember that for this strategy, you want to have a negative outlook on the chosen stock. You want a stock that will go down for some reason, whether you have heard some bad news about the stock or there is something else that will bring the value of your stock down.

After you have been able to pick out the right stock, you will need to purchase one slightly OOTM put option. You will also want to sell one OOTM put option, making sure that the strike price ends up being about one or two strikes lower than the option that you purchased in the first step. Additionally, ensure that you are picking out ones that have the same stock and the same expiry date as what you did with the first step.

Once you are done with all of these trades, you want to make sure that you monitor your position and watch what is going on. You will then want to get out of both positions once they have helped you to receive significant profit, which is about 30-40% of the maximum potential profit.

This one will work similarly to what you were able to do with the bull call spread. If you decide to increase the spread, you will increase how much potential profit you can make, but it also increases the risks that you are dealing with. Also, you can choose to decrease the spread, the risk will also decrease, but you would also limit how much profit you could potentially make on the trade.

There are a few times when you will choose to trade using the bear put spread. You will want to go with this kind of strategy when the market has a pretty negative outlook on the stock that you want to use. This is usually going to happen when some development occurs, such as the company not making the earnings that it should, or the organization has made some new changes or decisions that the investors did not look at favorably.

Some people choose to trade with this kind of strategy when the company is part of or is selling under pressure. They do not want to sell but there is something that is going on that will make them feel like they do need to sell. For example, there may be some environment or market conditions that are unfavorable to the company that surfaced and is changing the company.

Remember that since the bear put spread is considered a debit spread strategy, you will have to work with the time-decay and it will go against your overall position, even though this kind of decay is considered a lot slower than what will happen with a naked long put position.

When it comes to the disadvantages and advantages, this spread will end up being pretty similar to the bull call spread. The primary advantage that comes with this trade is that the ratio for risk and reward is pretty good and even a moderate decrease in stock can still help you to earn some good profits.

You will also be able to increase the amount of profit that you could potentially make by widening up the spread. To do this, you will want to increase the strike price that happens between your two options. You can also choose to reduce your risk to help you out as a beginner and to do this you will decrease the spread. To decrease the risk, you will want to decrease the number of strike prices that are going on between the two options.

The biggest disadvantage that comes with this strategy is dealing with the time decay that will work against the position. And while there is a limited amount of potential loss, if the stock ends up staying stagnant for a long period, the position will end up with a loss.

This one is pretty similar to the bull call spread, but it will end up having you invest oppositely. With this strategy, you will purchase a put option rather than the call option, at a specific strike price. Then when you see that the strike price goes lower, it is time to sell your option. This is a strategy that you would want to go with any time that you think the asset will go down in price. You will still make some kind of profit on it as long as the price does go down. However, if the price of the asset goes up, you could lose money in the process.

Chapter 15
THE BULL CALL SPREAD STRATEGY

Bull Call Spread

Profit

Long Call Strike Price

Short Call Strike Price

Price at Expiration

0

Loss

Now we will take a look at the bull call spread. This is another directional strategy that you can use any time that you have a positive outlook on your stock and you think that it will have a moderate rise in the short-term. As you will find with any of the other strategies that are spread based, both the potential losses and profits are capped when using the bull call spread. However, the best advantage of using this spread is that the maximum amount of profit that you will be able to gain from this strategy will exceed the maximum amount of loss that you may incur.

When you are working with this strategy, you will buy call options once a certain strike price has been reached. As soon as that strike price gets a little bit higher, you will turn around and sell that option, pocketing the difference as our profit. For this to work, you need to choose the right strike price so that you can earn a profit. This can be a good strategy to work with when you are looking at an option and you feel that the asset is about to go up. You can purchase it while it is still low and then take the profit that happens when it goes up.

The bull call spread is a bit different than the other strategies that we looked at because it is considered a debit spread. This means that you must pay what is known as a net debit to enter the position. This spread, as well as the bear put spread that we will talk about next, are the two strategies that you can choose that provide a high percentage of returns because they can be used to capitalize the momentum of the market while still making sure that the risk is as low as possible.

How can you get started with this strategy? First, you will want to pick out the stock that will meet all the criteria that you need to trade successfully with this strategy. Once you have chosen the strategy, you need to purchase one slightly OOTM call option.

Next, you need to sell one OOTM call option, but make sure that this call option has a strike price that is about one or two strikes higher than the option that you originally purchased. Both need to have the same expiry date and they need to be using the same stock.

After you have made both of the purchases that you would like, you need to make sure that you monitor your position and watch what the market is doing. It is a good idea to close up the position as soon as the trade has provided you with a good amount of profit. This will be when the profit reaches about 30-40%of the maximum amount that you can make on this trade.

You may be wondering when you should choose to use this kind of strategy when it comes to options trading. You will want to trade using the bull call spread whenever the market has a good outlook on whatever your chosen stock is. For example, if the stock of a company has received some positive news, like a good strategic move by the company, good earnings result, or some other news that would increase the growth of the stock.

You can also choose to work with the bull call spread on stocks that have been overcorrected and then have started showing strong signs of reversing. One thing to notice with this strategy is that since it works like a debit strategy, the time-decay will end up working against you. the decay will be much slower compared to working with a naked long call position, but the time-decay won't work as well as it did with the other options. This means that it is not the best idea to hold onto this spread for more than two or three weeks unless you see that the position keeps on gaining after the two weeks and that it is gaining a lot more than you expected.

If you enter this trade and notice that there isn't any momentum for the two weeks or more, it is best to exit out of the trade. You may end up taking a small loss when doing it, but at least you can free up your capital to use on other trades and you won't have to worry about losing more money out of the profit.

The main advantage of using this type of strategy is that there is a good ratio for your reward to risk and even a moderate move up in your stock could help you to make some good profits. You are also able to increase your potential for profits by widening up your spread, which means that you would increase the strike prices between your two options. You can also choose to reduce your risk a bit more by decreasing how many strike prices are between the two options. The method that you choose will depend on how much risk you would like to take and how favorable the market is.

You have to remember that you have to work against the time decay when you are working with this strategy. Despite the limited amount of loss potential with this strategy, if you are working with a stock that stays stagnant for a long time, the position will lose you money.

Chapter 16
THE ROLLING OUT OPTIONS STRATEGY

You want to avoid assignment →

EX. 1: ROLLING A CALL UP AND OUT	
Existing Position: 30-day 90-strike call	
Premium received	+$1.30
Premium paid to close 90-strike call	-$2.10
Premium received to open 60-day 95-strike call	+$2.30
Net credit from the roll	+$0.20

Here comes the roll

$1.30 initial premium + $0.20 net credit from roll = **+$1.50 net total** from this series of trades. (TradeKing commissions would be $11.20.)

A rollout is a strategy that is used to extend the lifetime of an option that hasn't quite worked out. This will be a strategy used by options sellers. So, a rollout might be something you would consider doing when you've sold a naked call, and the share price is closing in on your strike price, creating a risk that the option will be exercised. By doing a rollout you can keep the trade going longer, and possibly make some changes to give the trade better odds of being profitable. Typically, you will choose to do a rollout when it is close to the expiration date.

A rollout strategy works in the following way. You will close your current option contract by buying it back, and simultaneously open a new contract of the same type, with changes. One way to change is by altering the strike price. Another more common method is to move out of the expiration date. A common practice is to open the new contract with an expiration date that is further out in the future. So, for example, you could close a naked put option that is expiring in two days by buying it back and opening a new contract by selling a new naked put option. You would use the same stock and the same strike price, but with an expiration date that is three weeks into the future.

This is a standard strategy where we say that the option contract was rolled out.

You can also follow the same strategy choosing either a higher strike price or a lower strike price. For example, if we have an Apple naked put with a strike price of $205, we could roll up the option by closing this position and selling a new naked put on Apple with a strike price of $206. Alternatively, you could choose a lower strike price. Using the same example, instead of going with a $206 strike price, we could go with a $203 strike price. Maybe, in that case, the Apple share prices are dropping, and it got a little too close for comfort. When you select a lower strike price, they say that you have rolled down the trade.

It's also possible to roll out and roll up or down. In other words, you can close your current contract and open a new one that has a further expiration date, but you also change the strike price.

TYPES OF OPTIONS WHERE ROLLING STRATEGIES ARE USED

You can use a rollout, roll up, or roll down strategy on any type of option, including options that you buy to open (long calls and puts). However, the vast majority of options contracts that are rolled are short (buy to open) options. You can use rolling techniques on any of the major strategies covered in this book, such as credit spreads, strangles, or iron condors.

WHY ROLL AN OPTIONS CONTRACT?

The main reason that options traders roll an option contract is that they are in the money and there is an assignment risk. By rolling it out, you can keep the trade going but avoid assignment. Sometimes just moving the expiration date is good enough to accomplish this. An option can be assigned at any time, but in most cases, it has to reach expiration to be assigned. So by using a rollout, the trader can avoid this situation.

Of course, rolling up or rolling down can also help avoid assignment, since changing the strike price might allow you to move from an in the money situation to an out of the money situation.

Other reasons are sometimes used to justify rolling an option. For example, when you are selling for income, you can roll the trade to keep generating more money.

Changing market conditions might also be a reason to roll a trade.

When rolling a spread, strangle, or iron condor, many possibilities exist for altering the trade. Suppose you have a put credit spread with strikes of $207 and $204. We could change one or both of the strike prices, and we could also change the expiration date. Maybe we want to tighten or widen the spread, so we could roll out and also roll down the lower strike price and have a new spread with strike prices of $207 and $202, for example.

A ROLLOUT IS A SINGLE TRADE

It's important to note that a rollout is one trade, and not two. So, you are simultaneously closing one option (possibly with multiple legs) and opening a new contract in its place.

Chapter 17
MORE ABOUT OPTIONS STRATEGIES

In this chapter, we will talk a little bit more about options strategies, why they're important, how you can implement them well, and some common mistakes option traders make that are easily avoidable. We will then go on to discuss some common risks and how you can manage them efficiently. Let's begin now.

THE IMPORTANCE OF LEARNING ABOUT THESE STRATEGIES

The most attractive feature of options trading is the multitude of strategies it offers. There are a lot of factors that affect the potential outcome of a strategy. Some of them are Tax considerations, the cost involved in margin accounts, commission, and other transaction costs. Option strategies consider a lot of things. Whether the investor is a conservative or a growth-oriented or whether a short term and aggressive trader. The basic strategies form the foundation of more complex strategies.

Choosing the best entry and exit points of a position is a vital part of planning a trade. And this gets easy by using options strategies, particularly the simpler ones. To make options trading a profitable venture, maximizing your profit potential and limiting the potential loss becomes important. That can only be done by using different options strategies.

Choosing an appropriate options strategy makes the most out of your risks and regulates your subjection to risk. An advanced options trader with a lot of experience may even develop their strategy, but they need an options trading strategy, nonetheless. Beginners need to start with the more basic strategies and with time, try the more complex ones.

One should learn all they can about the most commonly used strategies and see how each of them works to know what advantages and disadvantages they have. No opportunity shall escape you once you can determine the most favorable strategy based on the existing conditions and your objectives.

COMMON MISTAKES TO AVOID WHEN WORKING WITH OPTION STRATEGIES

It is often said that in the options market, only 10% of the trades are winners. The success rate is very low, so the question is, what does it take to be a winning trader in the options market? The simplest thing you can do is avoid mistakes, the common ones at least. In this section, let's talk about some of these mistakes that traders often make in the options market. Avoiding these mistakes is the best way to avoid losses.

THE PRICE TAG PROBLEM

The first mistake we're going to discuss is also the one novice traders struggle the most with. As most of them have limited capital, deep OOTM options appeal a lot to them because they're so cheap. This stems from a misunderstanding of options results, and it's further compounded when these traders make an occasional winning trade and start getting even more fixated on deep OOTM options. Remember that the deeper the option is OOTM, the more it has to move for you to become profitable, and it has to do it fast because long term options are expensive. These sharp and quick moves are not typical of the market, so expecting success in this way is not a smart move and is quite risky. It's one of the biggest reasons beginning traders lose.

GETTING SWAYED BY EMOTIONS

Fear and greed are two of the primal emotions that human beings experience, and it's hard to separate ourselves from them when making trades. That is why these emotions are often referred to as a trader's biggest enemies. Greed can make you refuse to close your position when you're already profitable, or it can make you refuse to admit a lapse in judgment, which can lead to losses building up quickly. Similarly, fear can make you react the opposite way and bail out too quickly because you have no tolerance to risk. Always have a plan and make sure you stick to it when your emotions start acting up!

Even when traders are right, they often lose money when they don't have an exit plan because they don't understand the value of exiting on time. Having an exit plan is much more than just minimizing losses. It helps you establish patterns, trade more predictably, and control stress levels.

You need to have an upside and downside exit point prepared in advance, and you should also know about their appropriate timeframe. This is because the value of options decays with time. Trading can be exciting but keeping your emotions in check will be hugely beneficial for you.

ALLOCATE CORRECTLY

Most experienced traders will give you the time-tested advice that you should only commit 5% or less of your portfolio's worth in one single option trade. This is good advice, and here's another way to understand it. Say, you want to invest $20,000 in Microsoft. You can go ahead and buy MSFT shares worth $20,000. But for an option trader, this transaction would look a little different. She would buy enough option contracts that would control $20,000 in MSFT stock. This frees up a lot of capital for you to invest in a diversified portfolio.

DOUBLING UP TO MAKE UP FOR PAST LOSSES

Building upon our "emotions" mistake, let's talk about doubling up. Most traders have some sort of rules for themselves. It helps make life easier and decision-making more straightforward. You might make some of these rules for yourself, but they can easily go to the dogs when you find yourself in a bad situation.

We keep going forward with a losing trade, thinking to ourselves, "Hey, the entire market might be wrong about this, and I might be right. Wouldn't that be nice?"

If you've previously been a stock trader, you might even have heard the advice to double up so you can catch up easier. This makes it very appealing to buy more shares when the price drops lower and lower. But remember, you're not trading stocks anymore. What makes sense stocks often doesn't make sense for options, because they are derivatives and their prices move very differently from those of the underlying stocks.

Doubling up can seem tempting because it lowers the per-contract cost of your entire position, but it also compounds the risk. Therefore, doubling up is often a losing strategy in options, and you should avoid digging a deeper hole for yourself. If you wouldn't have invested more money if you didn't already have this position, why do it now? It's a trap you must avoid.

TRADING ILLIQUID OPTIONS

We know that there's always a difference between the bid price and the asking price of an option in the market. You'll notice the difference when you get a quote for any option first. Neither of these prices reflects the real value of the option, and it's usually in the middle somewhere. The liquidity of the option dictates how much the asking price and bid price will drift away from the real value. Liquidity simply means how many active traders are in the market for that option. There need always to be enough active buyers and sellers in the market for the option to be liquid. The more there are, the heavier the competition is, resulting in the ask and bid prices coming closer together. Stocks will always be more liquid than options because all traders are only trading in that one stock whereas, in the options market, there are numerous contracts to choose from. They all have different expiration dates and strike prices.

This can become an even more severe issue for an option trader if the underlying stock isn't liquid enough. So, the least you can do is trade-in options where the underlying stock trades more than a million shares a day. Anything less than that and the stock, as well as the options, will be considered illiquid.

Another concept you need to take note of is "open interest". Simply put, open interest is the number of option contracts that exist for a particular stock. It needs to be at least 50 times what you want to trade. So, if you will buy 10 contracts, the minimum open interest needs to be 500 contracts for it to be acceptable liquid.

WAITING TOO LONG TO BUY BACK SHORTS

When it comes to shorts, the best advice is always to be ready to buy them back early. A trade that is going your way right now might not do so tomorrow. It's easy to fall into this trap and get lulled into a false sense of security, but trade can go south at any moment. You might want to squeeze an extra nickel out of the trade, or you might just be too cheap to pay the commission and get out. Whatever it is, be smart and don't wait unnecessarily to buy back shorts.

Avoid being cheap and remove your risk from the table. You can profit when possible, and when not possible, you can at least avoid or minimize losses. A good rule is to buy back your shorts immediately if you can keep at least 4/5ths of your initial gain. So as an example, if you sold your short start for $1 and a week before it expires you can buy it for 20 cents, don't be cheap, and try to save a measly 20 cents. It's not worth the risk to hang on for another week. Step on it as soon as you get the chance and buy back your short.

LACK OF UNDERSTANDING OPTIONS

This should go without saying, but you should always have a good understanding of how options function before you start trading. Many traders underestimate the complexities of trading options and jump into the market thinking they'll figure it out as they go. This is a horrible idea unless you have money to burn.

Take your time and understand why options move the way they do, what the math behind it is, how the Greeks play into this, what the role of underlying stocks is, and how to pick a winning trade with a good risk-reward ratio.

OVERTRADING

The fact that in the options market you can control a much larger amount of stock with the same money than you can in the stock market is a huge advantage. But it can also turn into a big disadvantage if you're not careful about this. Yes, you can make bigger gains with a much smaller amount of money, and overtrading seems very tempting. But it might give you a false sense of wealth, making you feel like you're worth much more than you are. This further results in your trading an even higher number of options. It's a vicious cycle, and you should avoid overtrading actively.

LACK OF UNDERSTANDING OF TIME DECAY

As we've already discussed, options lose their value with time. This is a big factor that leads to losses for retail traders because they don't understand the concept of time decay. The underlying stock needs to move sharp, fast, and in line with the associated option for the option's price to go up. This usually doesn't happen, so holding your position and grinding it out is often a loss. The value starts decaying faster and faster as the expiration date approaches. Option prices are cheaper during the time, so novice traders think it's a good idea to take new bets. They forget that it's only going to result in losses for them. And even if it seems like a small amount now, it adds up in the long run.

These are some of the common mistakes you should avoid at all costs. You will still make mistakes along the way as you learn and get better at trading, but you can at least learn from the experience of others and avoid the most common pitfalls. Learn from your mistakes and always try to form good habits, in trading and life.

TYPES OF RISKS

To become a better trader and a profitable one, an investor needs to figure out risk properly. When an investment gains value, the investor gets eager because they know leverage is possible in options. An aggressive option trader can make exponentially more than an investor on the same stock the option is based upon. It's all possible because of the leverage offered by options trading.

A good tried and tested advice would be to not invest more than 3% to 5% of your portfolio into a single trade.

Any investments have a certain amount of risk involved. But in options trading, the risk increases to a great extent. One needs to ascertain the advantages and disadvantages of the strategy they're planning to use. The various Greeks that have been discussed show the more advanced types of risks that are present in options trading like the Implied volatility and the unlimited risk potential of some strategies.

Major Events and significant happenings in the world also become an important factor in accounting the risks present. These can be the Release of earnings reports, election results, major political changes, the introduction of new legal or taxation provisions, and other similar events.

TIME MAY NOT ALWAYS BE YOUR FRIEND

The thing about options is-they expire. Most of them at zero value. Especially when you are holding long options, time becomes of utmost essence. The deterioration of the premium in options increases with the decrease in the time left till expiration. In the last few days, the rate of disintegration has increased exponentially.

PRICES CAN MOVE VERY QUICKLY

Options offer high leverage, and thus, prices can move swiftly. And unlike in stocks, the movement can be very big and in little time. Small changes in the stock can render big changes to the options because of factors like time left till expiration and the correlation between the stock price and the option's strike price.

NAKED SHORT POSITIONS HAVE MORE RISK POTENTIAL

Selling options without hedging the position can lead to great losses with chances of even limitless losses. Naked short means selling a put or call without securing it with cash or some other option position. One can sell puts or calls with other options or stock. When an investor shorts a stock, they are selling stock that has been borrowed and must be returned to the owner. There is no security to be borrowed in options, only the obligations.

When a naked call is sold, the risk is theoretically unlimited. One is liable for the difference between the strike price and the quantum of price movement above this price as there is a cap on how much the stock price can increase. On the other hand, when a naked open put is sold, the potential loss is equal to the strike price.

To have a long subjection to a stock at a good price, selling naked puts is the way to go. If a stock seems too costly, instead of going after the stock price, one can sell a put and thus collect the premium.

RISK MANAGEMENT

Risk management is one of the most important parts of options trading. Like with any other kind of investment, trading is inherently risky. There will always be some amount of risk involved, but the key to trading successfully is to manage your capital and risk carefully.

Everyone has a different risk tolerance threshold, and that's completely fine. You should never stretch yourself too thin. Only trade with money you can afford to lose. Let's look at some ways you can control and manage your risk efficiently.

USING YOUR TRADING PLAN

Having a detailed trading plan is very important as it lays down some basic rules and guidelines you will follow in your trading activities. This helps you manage your money and limit your exposure to risk. Your plan should include how much risk you're comfortable taking and how much capital you will invest. This way, you allocate a fixed amount to options trading and you never end up touching the money you can't afford to lose.

You can't eliminate emotions from trading, but what you can do is minimize the impact they have on your trades by putting rules in place. If you stick to your plan and use only the allocated amount of capital for trading, you avoid behaving irrationally and taking risks you can't afford to.

If you're generally conservative with your trades and it's been working fine for you, there's no reason for you to take higher risks suddenly. This is especially important when you make a few losing trades in a row. You might want to take a risky trade to recover past losses, but that's not a good idea. Remind yourself you have a trading plan in place for a reason.

USING OPTIONS SPREADS

We've covered various types of spreads in the book. This is because they're one of the most powerful tools to dissipate your risk. Spreads let you combine different positions using the same underlying stocks, thereby helping you create a more secure overall position. The upfront costs to enter a position can be daunting, but you can use spreads to reduce them and thereby minimize the amount you stand to lose. Yes, it also reduces the potential profits you could make, but that's just part of controlling risk. We've covered several types of spreads in the book all ready to help you take advantage of pretty much any market condition.

For example, if you use a bull call spread, you reduce your initial investment and hence, limit the amount of money you stand to lose. This is done by buying ITM calls on a stock and then writing OOTM calls on the same stock since they're cheaper.

Similarly, when entering short positions, you can reduce your risk by using a bull put spread. This is done by writing ITM puts on a particular stock and then buying cheaper OOTM puts on the same stock by using some of that upfront payment you received from writing the put options.

As you can see, spreads are excellent strategies for risk management.

PORTFOLIO DIVERSIFICATION

The most popular technique of risk management is Diversification. Investors using the buy and hold strategy are generally the users of this technique. The essence of diversification is spreading investments over various companies and sectors thus creating an equitable portfolio of stocks instead of concentrating all the investment at a single point. This makes it less subjected to risk than a portfolio, which is largely composed of a particular type of investment.

Diversification isn't meant in the same way for options, but it has its uses. Diversification is used in options trading in different ways by using a combination of various strategies and trading options that have a multitude of underlying assets. The options being used can be of different types too. For using diversification, you just don't rely on a single outcome but create several ways of creating profits.

USING OPTIONS ORDERS

There's a range of orders you can use to manage your risk easily. Besides the four main orders (buy-to-open, sell-to-close, sell-to-open, buy-to-close), there are a host of other orders we can use to manage our risk.

Let's see an example. It's typical for a market order to be filled automatically at the best price available, but this might not be a good price for you if the market is volatile. You can use limit orders here to set a minimum and maximum price. This way, you avoid selling or buying at a price you don't want to.

Similarly, you can use stop orders like market stop order or the limit stop order to control how you exit a position. This can help you avoid unmitigated losses or lock in profits you're comfortable cashing out at.

I advise you to read more about option orders here once you have gained some experience in options trading.

MONEY MANAGEMENT AND POSITION SIZING

Money management and risk management are closely entangled with each other.an investor has a certain amount available to invest and hence it is crucial to control your capital budget. To not run into a position of inability to make more trades, one should take into consideration the size of a single position.

Position sizing means specifying the amount of capital you're willing to invest in a certain position.

It's quite a simple tool to use. One must calculate what percent of their total invested capital is in each trade proposition. It is also kind of like diversification.

Chapter 18
TECHNICAL INDICATORS

Technical indicators come into play in options trading when you need to determine turning points for underlying stock and the trends that get them to this point. When used correctly, they can help to determine the optimal time to buy or sell and also predict movement cycles. In general, technical indicators are calculated based on the pricing pattern of the underlying stock. Relevant data includes highs and lows, opening price, volume, and closing price. They typically take into account the data regarding a stock's price from the past few periods, based on the charts the person who is doing the analyzing prefers.

This information is then used to identify trends that show what has been happening regarding a specific stock and then using past information to determine likely results for the future. Technical indicators come in both leading and lagging varieties. Indicators that lag are based on data that already exists and make it easier to determine if a trend is in the process of forming or if the stock in question is simply trading within a range. The stronger the trend that the lagging indicator pinpoints the greater the chance it will continue. They typically drop the ball when it comes to predicting potential pullbacks or rally points, however.

When it comes to leading indicators, they are mainly useful when you are looking to predict the point in the future where the price of a specific stock will crash or rally. More often than not, these are momentum indicators which, as the name implies, gauge the strength of the movement the underlying stock will undertake. Leading indicators tend to come in handy when you need to determine if the price the stock in question has reached is untenable in the long run and, if so, when the slowdown of the current trend is likely to occur. Because both oversold and overbought stocks are guaranteed to experience a pullback, knowing when this move will occur will come in handy more likely than not.

Both types of indicators are equally useful at different times, and often in conjunction with one another as you will frequently need to know both what types of trends are forming and when they are ultimately going to peter out if you will want to utilize most strategies successfully. In general, you will want to stick to a minimum of 3 indicators at all times.

THE MOVING AVERAGE CONVERGENCE DIVERGENCE INDICATOR(MACD)

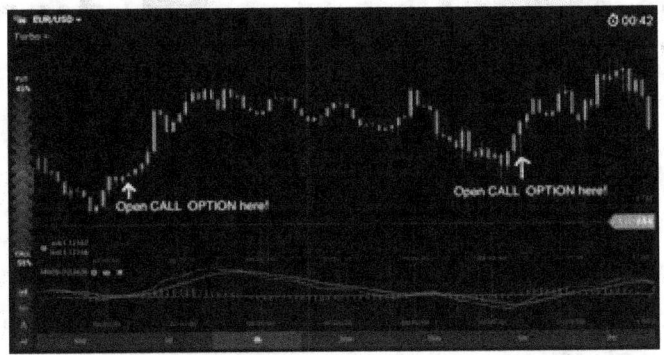

The moving average convergence divergence (MACD) indicator is a type of oscillating indicator that generally moves between the centerline and zero. If the MACD value is high, then this indicates the related stock is close to being overbought, and if the value is low then the stock is in danger of being oversold.

MACD charts are generally based on a combination of multiple exponential moving averages (EMAs). These averages can be based on any time frame, though the most common is the 12-26-9 chart. This chart is typically broken into multiple parts, the first of which is the 26-day and 12-day chart. Using an EMA that is slower or fast allows you to more accurately gauge the current momentum level for the trend you are currently keeping an eye on.

If the 12-day EMA, the fastest of the pair, ends up being above the 26-day EMA then you can safely assume that the underlying stock is in an uptrend while the reverse will also be the case. If the 12-day EMA increases at a rate that is greater than the 26-day EMA, then the uptrend is generally going to be even more pronounced. IF the 12-day EMA starts to move closer to the 26-day, then you can accurately assume that it is slowing down which means the momentum of the trade will fade. This, in turn, means you should expect the uptrend to end shortly.

The MACD puts these EMAs to use by considering the difference between them and then plotting it out. If the 26-day and the 12-day end up being the same, then the MACD will equal out to 0. If the 12-day ends up at a higher point than the 26-day, then the MACD will end up being positive. Otherwise, it will be negative. The larger the difference between them, the further the MACD line will fall from zero if the result is negative, or from the centerline if the result is positive.

By itself, this line does not provide any information that you would not be able to find from a simple moving average. However, it becomes much more useful once the 9-day EMA is taken into account as well. The 9-day EMA is different from the other 2 in that it shows the trend of the MACD line rather than the stock price. This means the 9-day EMA smooths out the movement of the MACD line to make its results more manageable.

In addition to the 9-day EMA, you are also going to want to look at the MACD histogram which looks at the difference between it and the base MACD line. When the MACD line crosses above the 9-day EMA, the MACD histogram will typically cross above 0 and thus indicate a bullish signal. If it crosses on the other side of 0, then you can take that to indicate a trend that will turn bearish if it has not already. When put to a chart, the histogram will form in a series of peaks that descends if the underlying stock is experiencing negative divergence and will generate a series of ascending peaks if it is experiencing positive divergence.

If the result generates a trend indicating negative divergence then you can feel relatively certain that the current positive trend will hit a level of resistance that it will not be able to overcome and, thus, reverse sooner than later. This can happen even if the pattern of the underlying stock has not started to run out of momentum quite yet. The same can be said about positive divergence and a negative trend. Remember the fact that these signals can become muddied if the price trades at or near the maximum range for a prolonged period. This means for the best results you are always going to want to use multiple indicators at once to prevent yourself from giving in to false signals.

THE AVERAGE DIRECTIONAL INDEX

The average directional index can be thought of as a guidepost that confirms the signals that other technical indicators bring to light. After a trend has been identified successfully, the average directional index can then more easily determine its strength compared to the other trends that are currently taking place. The average directional index is a combination of directional indicators that are both negative and positive and thus can more easily track trends regardless of their direction. They are then unified in a way that determines the overall strength of the trend.

As an oscillating indicator, the average directional index ranges between 100 and 0. The low end indicates that the trend is essentially flat and without volatility while the high end indicates that the stock is virtually moving straight up and down very quickly. This indicator is only useful when it comes to measuring the overall strength of the trend, not which direction it is moving in, or is likely to move in anytime soon.

As a general rule, it is rare to see an average directional index value above 60. This is because trends with that much strength are only likely to appear in periods of a deep recession or extremely long bullish market runs. What this means is that a value of anything greater than 40 can be considered a vibrant trend and anything lower than 20 indicates an underlying stock within a trading range.

When watching for average directional index signals, if a trend moves from above 40 to below it, then you can assume the current trend is slowing which means it may be time to mix up your current trading strategy or close out any existing positions. However, if you see a trend start at less than 20 and then increase to a point near 40 then you will know that a neutral market is starting to pick up steam and a major trend is likely going to be formed.

It is also important to always keep in mind the point where the negative directional index and the positive directional index cross. If the negative directional index is crossed by the positive in an upward direction, then you can assume the market is feeling bullish. If things happen the other way, then you can expect bearish trends instead.

THE RELATIVE STRENGTH INDEX

The relative strength index (RSI) is another type of momentum indicator that compares the relative magnitude of recent losses when compared to recent gains as a means of determining if a given stock is oversold or overbought. This, in turn, allows it to generate vital indications about the correlating reversals or corrections that are forthcoming, making price movements in the short-term clearer. RSI is most effective when used to measure individual stocks as opposed to indexes because it is more likely the individuals will experience either condition.

RSI values range from 0 to 100. Any value above 70 shows the stock is overbought and anything under 30 shows it is undersold. In general, options that are on high beta stocks with high liquidity will provide the best RSI results.

Some traders find that the RSI provides the most effective information when it is compared to crossovers with the short-term moving average. With the help of a 25-day and a 10-day moving average, you will likely be able to easily discern crossovers that show that a direction shift will occur in periods where the RSI is either in the range of 80 and 20 or 70 and 30. Regardless of what it shows, the RSI is always going to indicate a period of reversal, regardless of the precise direction.

The concept known as failure swings can make it easier for investors to take full advantage of the information shown through an RSI. Remember that just because the RSI shows either something in the range of 30 or 70, does not mean that the reversal will happen right away. Rather, positions can remain in overbought or oversold positions for an extended period. When the RSI extends to these levels, you will want to start watching the volume indicators to make it clear when traders start taking profits at the top or building up at the bottom. To make the most of this tool, it may be helpful to study old charts as a means of determining the types of price action you are likely to see at the opposite ends of an RSI, so you know what to expect.

BOLLINGER BAND

The importance of volatility when it comes to correctly valuing an option is well known. This is why Bollinger bands are so useful as they make it easy to grasp this facet of a particular stock, in turn, making it easier to identify lower and upper ranges. They work by generating bands based on the way the stock price has recently been moving. Bollinger bands trend to provide 2 types of indications:

The bands tend to contract and expand depending on how volatility decreases or increases based on the way the price has been moving recently. If the bands expand then volatility is increasing, if they contract then volatility is decreasing. With this in mind, you can feel safer taking on reversal based option positions.

The range of the current band can also be compared to the current market price as a means of determining any potential breakout patterns. If the breakout occurs at the top of the band, then you know the market has been overbought which means it is time to buy puts or short existing calls. If the breakout occurs at the bottom of the lower band, then you know the market is oversold which means it is time to buy short puts or calls that come with lower overall volatility.

Either way, it is important to take care to assure the current volatility as shorting options if volatility is high can be beneficial. It can lead to higher premiums if volatility is high and cheaper options if volatility is low. The best value for a Bollinger band is up to the trader. However, the most commonly used value is 2 for the standard deviation of the top and bottom bands and 12 for the simple moving average.

The squeeze is the core concept of Bollinger bands as when the bands come close together they constrict the moving average and squeeze it tight, hence the name. A squeeze indicates that the volatility will be low for a time while the future likelihood will be increased, as will the number of potentially profitable opportunities to trade. On the other hand, the wider the bands end up being, the greater the likelihood of decreased volatility and the higher the likelihood that it is time to exit the trade. Always note that these two conditions are not trading signals in the traditional sense. The bands themselves give no true indication of what direction the price is likely to move in or when the potential change will take place.

Overall, Bollinger bands are not designed to be used in a vacuum. Rather, they are better served as an additional indicator which can then provide traders with additional information when it comes to the volatility of the price. Ideally, you will want to use them with at least 2 other indicators that are non-correlated and also provide more direct market signals. Using Bollinger bands under these circumstances will help you to discover opportunities that you may have otherwise missed with an overall higher degree of success.

INTRADAY MOMENTUM INDEX

If you tend to trade options more frequently than the average trader you will want to pay attention to the intraday momentum Index (IMI) as it is a useful indicator when it comes to intraday trades. It utilizes candlesticks along with an RSI to create a useful intraday trading range by showing off oversold and overbought markets. Take into account how trendy these price moves areas if there is a visible, strong trend then the indicator might give off a false positive and read it as an oversold or overbought opportunity.

If you are aware of these trends, and also make use of the IMI, then you will have the ability to spot these types of incidents sooner than you otherwise would, making it possible to get into an early long position while the market is still on the uptrend or get into a short position if it is in a downtrend. You can determine the IMI with the following calculation.

If Close > Open: Gains = Gain (n-1) + (Close - Open); Losses = 0

If Close < Open: Losses = Loss (n-1) + (Open - Close); Gains = 0

Add Gains and Losses for past n chosen periods

IMI = 100 x (Gains / (Gains + Losses))

When combined with the possibility of leverage, the IMI can be a profitable technical indicator to use while you are trading options. The formula is also flexible in that each trader can use the n value that suits them best. Commonly used values include 70 or above for overbought markets and 30 or less for markets that are oversold.

MONEY FLOW INDEX

If you are looking for a type of technical indicator to use as a complement to the RSI, the money flow index is a reliable choice. It combines volume and price data as a means of identifying price trends in a given stock. It is also known sometimes called the volume-weighted RSI. As volume is taken into consideration, this indicator can generate useful inputs regarding the amount of capital moving into and out of the chosen stock over a set period. The most commonly used time frame is 14 days.

PUT CALL RATIO INDICATOR

The put-call ratio indicator (PCR) is useful when you need to determine the volume of call or put options that a given stock has attached to it. Rather than dealing in absolute value, the PCR indicates when the market's sentiment is changing. The greater the change in its value, the greater the change in the market as a whole. If the value drops, then this indicates a bullish trend which means more calls are being used. Likewise, a value that increases in value will show a trend towards bearishness and more puts overall.

As it is dependent on data regarding volume, the MFI indicator is especially useful for options trading based on stocks as opposed to indices. It is also known to see better results for longer forms of options trading than with intraday trading. In general, you will want to look for scenarios where the MFI indicator moves away from the stock price as this is generally a leading indicator that signals a trend reversal is coming. The best values to base your predictions on are 20 for oversold and 80 for overbought.

There are two primary types of financial instruments, these include the primary securities and instruments as well as other instruments whose value is wholly derived based on their relationship to the primary instruments. When it comes to options, those underlying assets are securities which are what this indicator is looking at.

Chapter 19
FUNDAMENTAL ANALYSIS

Depending on who you ask, fundamental analysis can be thought of as the cornerstone of profitable trading. Even with that in mind, however, it can be difficult for those new to analyze in general to get a clear idea of where they should start. This part, at least, is relatively straightforward as a major part of fundamental analysis revolves around looking into financial statements related to the underlying assets that you are following.

Referred to as quantitative analysis, this aspect of fundamental analysis means looking at things like liabilities, assets, expenses, and revenue to determine how the related asset is likely going to look in the relatively near, or distant, future. As a fledgling fundamental analyst. You must understand the importance of various economic indicators and how they all come together to form a single picture, and the following chapters will aim to do just that.

Fundamental analysis is more than just staring at the numbers, however, which is why in addition to quantitative analysis, you will also need to learn about qualitative analysis which is all about breaking down the intangible qualities that make a company a success. When used in conjunction with one another they can provide a very clear picture of the viability of certain options and, ideally, point to instances of specific assets being valued below where they should be.

When it comes to analyzing the fundamentals of specific underlying assets, you will need to start by establishing a baseline so that you have a good idea of when things start to change. To determine a baseline, you will want to start by considering relevant issues to ensure you gather the right type of data that is actively affecting the assets in question. You will also want to consider the way that the assets have behaved in the past as previous behavior is often a solid indicator of the future as well.

Additionally, when it comes to gathering past data you will want to determine the current phase that the asset is in. Each asset has three phases, if the related currency is booming then liquidity will be high, and volatility will be low; if it is in a bust period then liquidity will be low and volatility will be high. Additionally, assets can be in a pre or post bust phase as well as a pre or post-boom phase. Accurately picking out the current phase is a key to becoming a successful trader and finding profit where others miss out on the profits that you found easily.

As a general rule, lower numbers are an indicator of a stronger market, but if the market has been strong for too long, then you know a bust is likely on the way and will need to plan accordingly. The market is often slow to react to these types of things which means that taking advantage of them early and often can lead to big payouts sooner than later.

Once you have a clear idea of the current state of things, the next thing you will want to focus on are sectors that you feel will experience major growth as the current boom or bust phase plays itself out. This could be things like new technology, new market fundamentals, or new political leanings as well as a host of similar scenarios; regardless, finding scenarios that lead to an increase in productivity is a great way to home in on opportunities that you can ensure are on the qualitative target.

Technology is always a great factor to consider as the moment that a new technology catches on in the mainstream is always going to be followed by an increase in productivity, which will, in turn, lead to an increase in demand for the technology which leads to positive growth in the market. Likewise, the political climate of various regions can have a direct influence on underly assets of all types that may otherwise not appear to be related to the political issue in question. As a general rule, the greater the overall global tension, the greater the amount of volatility and the less liquidity you are likely to find. As such, the qualitative quality of an underlying asset should be directly proportional to how mild the political climate in the region currently is.

QUANTITATIVE AND QUALITATIVE ANALYSIS

Fundamental analysis is all about researching the fundamentals of a given company, but that alone won't be enough to tell you what you need to know unless you know what fundamentals you are working with to start. Unfortunately, this can be more comprehensive than you might hope as the fundamentals can include practically anything that affects the economic viability of your chosen company in one way or another. Fundamentals include things such as profit or revenue, but they can also include things like the quality of its leadership and its market share.

Generally speaking, different fundamental factors can be classified in two ways, quantitative and qualitative. Quantitative factors are those that are purely numerical, things that will be written down and discussed during the next investors' meeting. Qualitative factors are those that focus more on the inherent qualities of the company and the things that make it great, which naturally makes them more difficult to track. Qualitative factors are generally less tangible and include things like its name recognition, the patents it holds, and the quality of its board members.

Neither of these types of factors will naturally be superior to the together, and they will typically provide better results when they are used in conjunction with one another. For example, consider the Coca-Cola Company. For quantitative factors, an analyst could look at its P/E ratio, earnings per share, and, of course, its annual dividend payout rate. For qualitative factors, you would need to consider its overall brand recognition which takes it from a company that essentially sells carbonated sugar water to a company that is recognized by almost everyone on the planet. While this figure can't be quantified with a dollar amount it is, without a doubt, one of the major contributing factors to its overall success.

IMPORTANT QUALITATIVE FACTORS TO CONSIDER

BUSINESS MODEL

The first thing that you will want to do when you catch wind of a company that might be worth following up on is to check out its business model which is more or less a generalization of how it makes its money. You can typically find these sorts of details on the company website or in its 10-K filing.

COMPETITIVE ADVANTAGE

It is also important to consider the various competitive advantages that the company you have your eye on might have over its competition. Companies that are successful in the long-term are always going to have an advantage over their competition in one of two ways. They can either have better operational effectiveness or improved strategic positioning. Operational effectiveness is the name given to doing the same things as the competition but more efficiently and effectively. Strategic positioning occurs when a company gains an edge by doing things that nobody else is doing.

LEADERSHIP

The type of management that is currently leading a company will go a long way towards determining if it will be successful in the long run. After all, even the most well thought out business plan will fail without being able to rely on the right infrastructure to support it in the long run. When it comes to analyzing management, the first place you will want to look at is the corporate information section of the company's website. This won't provide you with much more than the names of the folks at the top, but if they have been around the block then names should be enough to pull up everything you need to know about their past work experiences. While this might not ultimately amount to much if there is something unfortunate in their past this should bring it to light.

IMPORTANT QUANTITATIVE FACTORS TO CONSIDER

The sheer volume of data and the large number of varying numbers found in the average company's financial statements can easily be intimidating and bewildering for conscientious investors who are digging into them for the first time. Once you get the hang of them, however, you will quickly find that they are a goldmine of information when it comes to determining how likely a company is to continue producing reliable dividends in the future.

BALANCE SHEET

A balance sheet shows a detailed record of all of a company's equity, liabilities, and assets for a given period. A balance sheet shows a balance to the financial structure of a company by dividing the company's equity by the combination of shareholders and liabilities to determine its current assets.

CASH FLOW STATEMENT

A cash flow statement typically shows the complete record of the cash outflow and inflow for a specific company over a specified length of time. The cash flow statement is especially important as it is more difficult for businesses to manipulate than some of its other financial documents. While it might be possible for accountants to manipulate earnings, it is much harder to fake cash in the bank. This is why many investors consider the cash flow statement a more reliable measure of a company's current performance.

INCOME STATEMENT

While the balance sheet can be thought of as a snapshot of the fundamental economic aspects of the company, an income statement takes a closer look at the performance of the company exclusively for a given timeframe. There is no limit to the length of time an income statement considers, which means you could see them generated month to month, or even day to day; however, the most common type used by public companies are either annual or quarterly. Income statements provide information on profit, expenses, and revenues that resulted from the business that took place over a specific period.

Chapter 20
TECHNICAL ANALYSIS

When it comes to understanding technical analysis, the most important thing to always keep in mind is that the action that a certain price has taken in the past is likely going to be a reliable way to predict its action in the future. This fact then makes it easy to use what are known as technical tools, things like indicators, charts, and trends to achieve a reliable rate of success that successful traders require. While the ways it can do so can be quite complicated at times, at its heart, technical analysis studies supply and demand to decide what trend, if any, is likely going to continue moving forward. This is crucial for long term success as the tools that technical analysis provides will increase the reliability of each of your trades nearly every single time.

The goal of technical analysis is not to simply measure the given intrinsic value of a particular asset, but rather to use the tools at your disposal to pick out beneficial patterns related to a future activity that others may not yet have noticed. At its core, technical analysis functions by assuming three things to be true. First, the market will always discount anything; second, prices will always move according to trends; and finally, history will always repeat itself eventually. What follows are several charts and patterns to consider when utilizing the strategies.

Technical analysis is the method of using charts and other recording methods to analyze various data in options trading. Using these visual instruments, you have the chance to determine the direction of the market because they give you a trend.

This method focuses on studying the supply and demand of a market. The price will be seen to rise when the investor realizes the market is undervalued, and this leads to buying. If they think that the market is overvalued, the prices will start falling, and this is deemed the perfect time to sell.

You need to understand the movement of the various indicators to make the perfect decision. This method works on the premise that history usually repeats itself – a huge change in the prices affects the investors in any situation.

HISTORY

Technical analysis has been used over the years in trades. The technical analysis methods have been used for over a hundred years to come up with deductions regarding the market.

In Asia, the use of technical analysis led to the development of candlestick techniques, and it forms the main charting techniques. Over time, more tools and techniques have come up to help traders come up with predictions of the prices in various markets.

There are many indicators that you can use to determine the direction of the market, but only a few are valuable to your course. Let us look at the various indicators and how to use them.

THE SIGNIFICANCE OF TRENDS IN OPTION TRADING

Technical analysis works on the premise of the trend. These trends come by due to the interaction of the buyer and the seller. The aggressiveness of one of the parties in the market will determine how steep the trend becomes. To make a profit, you have to take advantage of the changes in the price movement.

To understand the direction of the trend, you ought to look at the troughs and peaks and how they relate to each other.

When looking for money in options trading, you ought to trade with a trend. The trend is what determines the decision you make when faced with a situation – whether to buy or to sell. You need to know the various signs that a prevailing trend is soon ending so that you can manage the risks and exit the trades the right way.

CHARACTERISTICS OF TECHNICAL ANALYSIS

This analysis makes use of models and trading rules using different price and volume changes. These include the volume, price, and other different market info.

Technical analysis is applied among financial professionals and traders and is used by many option traders.

THE PRINCIPLES OF TECHNICAL ANALYSIS

Many traders on the market use the price to come up with information that affects the decision you make ultimately. The analysis looks at the trading pattern and what information it offers you rather than looking at drivers such as news events, economic and fundamental events.

Price action usually tends to change every time because the investor leans towards a certain pattern, which in turn predicts trends and conditions.

PRICES DETERMINE TRENDS

Technical analysts know that the price in the market determines the trend of the market. The trend can be up, down, or move sideways.

HISTORY USUALLY REPEATS ITSELF

Analysts believe that an investor repeats the behavior of the people that traded before them. The investor sentiment usually repeats itself. Since the behavior repeats itself, traders know that using a price pattern can lead to predictions.

The investor uses the research to determine if the trend will continue or if the reversal will stop eventually and will anticipate a change when the charts show a lot of investor sentiment.

COMBINATION WITH OTHER ANALYSIS METHODS

To make the most out of the technical analysis, you need to combine it with other charting methods on the market. You also need to use secondary data, such as sentiment analysis and indicators.

To achieve this, you need to go beyond pure technical analysis and combine other market forecast methods in line with technical work. You can use technical analysis along with fundamental analysis to improve the performance of your portfolio.

You can also combine technical analysis with economics and quantitative analysis. For instance, you can use neural networks along with technical analysis to identify the relationships in the market. Other traders make use of technical analysis with astrology.

Other traders go for newspaper polls, sentiment indicators to come with deductions.

THE DIFFERENT TYPES OF CHARTS USED IN TECHNICAL ANALYSIS

CANDLESTICK CHART

This is a charting method that came from the Japanese. The method fills the interval between opening and closing prices to show a relationship. These candles use color-coding to show the closing points. You will come across black, red, white, blue, or green candles to represent the closing point at any time.

OPEN-HIGH-LOW-CLOSE CHART (OHLC)

These are also referred to as bar charts, and they give you a connection between the maximum and minimum prices in a trading period. They usually feature a tick on the left side to show the open price and one on the right to show the closing price.

LINE CHART

This is a chart that maps the closing price values using a line segment.

POINT AND FIGURE CHART

This employs numerical filters that reference times without fully using the time to construct the chart.

OVERLAYS

These are usually used on the main price charts and come in different ways:

RESISTANCE

Refers to a price level that acts as the maximum level above the usual price

SUPPORT

The opposite of resistance, and it shows the lowest value of the price

TREND LINE

This is a line that connects two troughs or peaks.

CHANNEL

Refers to two trend lines that are parallel to each other

MOVING AVERAGE

A kind of dynamic trendline that looks at the average price in the market

BOLLINGER BANDS

These are charts that show the rate of volatility in a market.

PIVOT POINT

This refers to the average of the high, low, and closing price averages for a certain stock or currency.

PRICE-BASED INDICATORS

These analyze the price values of the market. These include:

ADVANCE DECLINE LINE

This is an indicator of the market breadth

AVERAGE DIRECTIONAL INDEX

Shows the strength of a trend in the market

COMMODITY CHANNEL INDEX

Helps you to identify cyclical trends in the market

RELATIVE STRENGTH INDEX

This is a chart that shows you the strength of the price

MOVING AVERAGE CONVERGENCE (MACD)

This shows the point where two trend lines converge or diverge.

STOCHASTIC OSCILLATOR

This shows the close position that has happened within the recent trading range

MOMENTUM

This is a chart that tells you how fast the price changes

THE BENEFITS OF TECHNICAL ANALYSIS IN OPTIONS TRADING

EXPERT TREND ANALYSIS

This is the biggest advantage of technical analysis in any market. With this method, you can predict the direction of the market at any time. You can determine whether the market will move up, down, or sideways easily.

ENTRY AND EXIT POINTS

As a trader, you need to know when to place a trade and when to opt-out. The entry point is all about knowing the right time to enter the trade for good returns. Exiting a trade is also vital because it allows you to reduce losses.

LEVERAGE EARLY SIGNALS

Every trader looks for ways to get early signals to assist them in making decisions. Technical analysis gives you signals to trigger a decision on your part. This is usually ideal when you suspect that a trend will reverse soon. Remember the time the trend reverses is when you need to make crucial decisions.

IT IS QUICK

In options trading, you need to go with techniques that give you fast results. Additionally, getting technical analysis data is cheaper than other techniques in fundamental analysis, with some companies offering free charting programs. If you are in the market to make use of short time intervals such as 1-minute, 5-minute, 30 minute, or 1-hour charts, you can get this using technical analysis.

IT GIVES YOU A LOT OF INFORMATION

Technical analysis gives you a lot of information that you can use to make trading decisions. You can easily build a position depending on the information you get then take or exit trades. You have access to information such as chart patterns, trends, support, resistance, market momentum, and other information.

YOU UNDERSTAND TRENDS

Trends run in various degrees. The degree of the trend determines how much money you make, whether in the short term or long-term trading. Technical analysis gives you all the tools that make it possible for you to do this.

HISTORY ALWAYS REPEATS ITSELF

Technical analysis uses common patterns to give you the information to trade. However, you need to understand that history will not be exact when it repeats itself, though. The current analysis will be either bigger or smaller, depending on the existing market conditions. The only thing is that it won't be a replica of the prior pattern.

ENJOY PROPER TIMING

Do you know that without proper timing you will not be able to make money at all? One of the major advantages of technical analysis is that you get the chance to time the trades. Using technical analysis, you get to wait, then place your money in other opportunities until it is the right time to place a trade.

APPLICABLE OVER A WIDE TIME FRAME

When you learn technical analysis, you get to apply it to many areas in different markets, including options. All the trading in a market is based mostly on the patterns that are a result of human behavior. These patterns can then be mapped out on a chart to be used across the markets.

TECHNICAL ANALYSIS SECRETS TO BECOME THE BEST TRADER

To make use of technical analysis the right way, you need to follow time-testing approaches that have made the technique a gold mine for many traders. Let us look at the various tips that will take you from novice to pro in just a few days:

USE MORE THAN ONE INDICATOR

Numbers make trading easy, but it also applies to the way you apply your techniques. For one, you need to know that just because one technical indicator is better than using one, applying a second indicator is better than using just one. The use of more than one indicator is one of the best ways to confirm a trend. It also increases the odds of being right.

As a trader, you will never be 100 percent right at all times, and you might even find that the odds are stashed against you when everything is plain to see. However, don't demand too much from your indicators such that you end up with analysis paralysis.

To achieve this, make use of indicators that complement each other rather than the ones that clash against each other.

GO FOR MULTIPLE TIME FRAMES

Using the same buy signal every day allows you to have confidence that the indicator is giving you all you need to know to trade. However, make sure you look for a way to use multiple timeframes to confirm a trend. When you have a doubt, it is wise that you increase the time frame from an hour to a day or from a daily chart to a weekly chart.

UNDERSTAND THAT NO INDICATOR MEASURES EVERYTHING

You need to know that indicators are supposed to show how strong a trend is, they won't tell you much more. So, you need to understand and focus on what the indicator is supposed to communicate instead of working with assumptions.

GO WITH THE TREND

If you notice that an option is trading upward, then go ahead and buy it. Conversely when the trend stops trending, then it is time to sell it. If you aren't sure of what is going on in the market at that time, then don't make a move.

However, waiting might make you lose profitable trades as opposed to trading. You also miss out on opportunities to create more capital.

HAVE THE RIGHT SKILLS

It takes superior analytical capabilities and real skill to be successful at trading, just like any other endeavor. Many people think that it is hard to make money with options trading, but with the right approach, you can make extraordinary profits.

You need to learn and understand the various skills so that you know what the market seeks from you and how to achieve your goals.

TRADE WITH A PURPOSE

Many traders go into options trading with the main aim of having a hobby. Well, this way you won't be able to make any money at all. What you need to do is to trade for the money – strive to make profits unlike those who try to make money as a hobby.

ALWAYS OPT FOR HIGH VALUE

Well, no one tells you to trade any security that comes your way – it is purely a matter of choice. Try and go for high-value options so that you can trade them the right way. Make use of fundamental analysis to choose the best options to trade-in.

BE DISCIPLINED

When using technical analysis, you might find yourself in situations that require you to make a decision fast. To achieve success, you need to have strict risk management protocols. Don't base on your track record to come up with choices; instead, make sure you follow what the analysis tells you.

DON'T OVERLOOK YOUR TRADING PLAN

The trading plan is in place to guide you when things go awry. Coming up with the plan is easy, but many people find it hard to implement the plan the right way. The trading plan has various components — the signals and the take-profit/stop-loss rules. Once you get into the market, you need to control yourself because you have already leaped. Remember you cannot control the indicators once they start running — all you can do is to prevent yourself from messing up everything.

Come up with the trading rules when you are unemotional to try and mitigate the effects of making bad decisions.

ACCEPT LOSSES

Many people trade with one thing in mind — losses aren't part of their plan. This is a huge mistake because you need to understand that every trade has two sides to it — a loss and a profit. Remember that the biggest mistake that leads to losses isn't anything to do with bad indicators rather using them the wrong way. Always have a stop-loss order when you trade to prevent loss of money.

HAVE A TARGET WHEN YOU TRADE

So, what do you plan to achieve today? Remember, trading is a way to grow your capital as opposed to saving. Options trading is a business that has probable outcomes that you get to estimate. When you make a profit, make sure you take some money from the table and then put it in a safe place.

HOW TO APPLY TECHNICAL ANALYSIS

Many traders have heard of technical analysis, but they don't know how to use it to make deductions and come up with decisions that impact their trades. Here are the different steps to make sure you have the right decision when you use technical analysis.

IDENTIFY A TREND

You need to identify an option and then see whether there is a trend or not. The trend might be driving the options up or down. The market is bullish if it is moving up and bearish when it is moving down. As a trader, you need to go along with the trend instead of fighting it. When you fight against the trend, you incur unnecessary losses that will make it hard to achieve the rewards that you seek.

You also need to have good ways to identify the trend; this is because the market can move in a certain direction. It is not all about identifying the direction of the trend but also when the trend is moving out of the trend.

So, how can you identify a trend the right way? Here are some tools to use to get the right trend:

• Using triangles that map major swings

• The Bill Williams Fractals indicator helps you to identify the trend

• Use the moving average

• Trend lines give you an idea of the direction of the trend

Once you identify the trend, the next step is to try and mark the support and resistance levels

SUPPORT AND RESISTANCE LEVELS

You need to understand the support and resistance levels that are within the trend. Use the Fibonacci retracement tool to identify these spots on the trend.

LOOK FOR PATTERNS

Patterns need to show you what to expect in a certain market. You can use candlesticks to determine the chart pattern.

Chapter 21
SUPPORT AND RESISTANCE

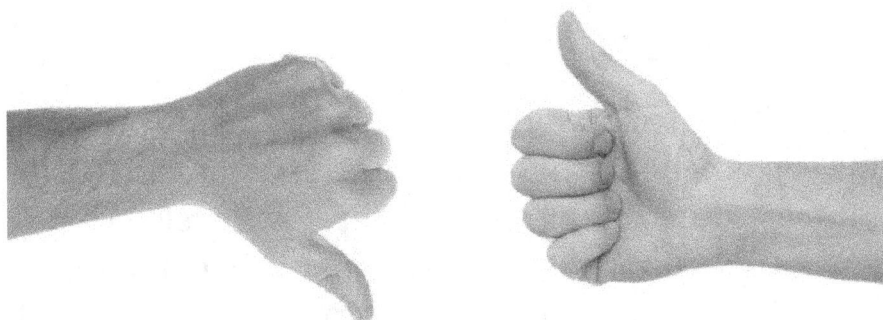

These levels occur at points where both the buyer and the seller aren't dormant. These levels are displayed on the chart using a horizontal line extended in the past to the future.

The different prices reach the support and resistance points in the future.

HOW TO APPLY SUPPORT AND RESISTANCE

Support and resistance give you a way to determine the entry point to use for a directional trade.

Support and resistance levels, on the surface, seem as simple to decipher as trends. After all, much like looking left to right, simply mark whichever level price has bounced from and that's it, right? Well, if it were that simple, trading would be the easiest thing in the world and there would be no need for books like this one.

This is not to say that S/R is complicated. Far from it. What trips up most traders is not their ability to spot levels but their mindset in locating them as we'll shortly see.

ORDER FLOW LEVELS

Instead of designating the levels price bounces from as support and resistance, a more accurate term would be to call them order flow levels. This is because when viewed from an order flow perspective, it's a whole lot easier to understand which level will play an important role and why.

You see, the default method of S/R is to only look at price levels in the past and ignore what it is doing currently. There's no taking into account the counter-trend distribution or the current bias of the market. All of these play a very important role in determining what will act as an S/R level shortly, from where the price will have a reaction you can take advantage of.

HOW S/R IS FORMED

As price moves in a given direction, buyers and sellers interact and leave an imprint for everyone to see. In some cases, one side overwhelms the other and, in some cases, both sides reach a mutual agreement over a certain price point. There are some areas on the chart which are more suitable for such mutual agreement than others.

Why would traders agree on such price points? Well, the causes are numerous. Perhaps there was some fundamental event that took place or perhaps this number has some sort of psychological significance. Perhaps, some traders cornered the market and thought it would be funny. This doesn't happen anymore, thanks to the size of the stock market but every once in a while, you will see such shenanigans on the commodities markets. Such occurrences are more frequent than you might think on the bond markets.

Speaking of which, bond markets have an impact on the stock market as well. The bond markets are entirely institutional and are about ten times the size of the stock market. A lot of hedge funds and banks place bets on the stock market via derivatives in the bond market and thus, the ripple effect is felt in stocks.

My point is this: No one knows why a level is important. It isn't your job to determine why a level is important. What you need to figure out is, which level do the largest number of trader's think is important. Thus, the importance of a level is directly tied to the current order flow characteristics.

If the bears are heavily dominant, would they consider a level where they previously fought off the bulls important? Or would they consider a level where the bulls fought back earnestly as more important? There's no straightforward or formulaic answer to this. Much like with the rest of the market, all we have is probabilities.

The best we can do is identify patterns of support and resistance and see how traders treat prior price reaction points concerning current order flow and project how they might react in the future. All of this sounds more complicated than it is. However, a point I'd like to emphasize here is that there's no gain in you defining set rules for yourself when it comes to S/R.

A lot of beginners come in with weird rules like "the prior swing high is not as important as the prior swing low in a bull trend retest" and so on. Well, every bull trend's order flow characteristics are different and there's no way we can know in advance or hypothetically how something will behave. The best way to form a decision is to look at a chart and draw conclusions based on what you see.

So, let go of the rules or even your need for them. It is counter-intuitive but letting go of rules will result in your trading in a far more disciplined manner since you're now in line with the true nature of the market, which is to respect the odds and not seek certainty over every single thing.

ZONES

The first lesson for you to learn is that price levels are not single horizontal lines like they're depicted in charts but zones. Remember, the market is made of traders placing orders. There are traders on your time frame, on time frames multiple levels below you, and above you. It's unrealistic to think that all these millions of traders will think of a single number as being the definitive support or resistance level. So, when looking for S/R, look for zones, not simple horizontal lines.

The biggest indicator of a good S/R level is the amount of order flow it has seen. Indications of heavy order flow are multiple touches, prolonged testing of a level, and so on. The further away the tests of the level are from one another, the better. From an order flow perspective, this indicates that traders believe this level contains support for a given side of the market over time and this isn't just a short-term fad.

Figure 4: Strong S/R Zones

Figure 4 illustrates the strong support and resistance zones simultaneously. This is a characteristic of ranges. The instrument is the FTSE 100 and the timeframe is the daily chart. Notice on the bottom, that after the initial double dips in August and mid-September (themselves a month apart), the price dips back into this level in mid-December and is still respected. In the new year, despite a strong bearish push into the bottom, the level still holds for a few days before breaking down.

On top, the hits are not as far apart as on the bottom but they're still numerous. October through November sees the FTSE constantly pushing against the top but without any success. Then, the December push up also gets rejected.

Figure 4 gives us a handy lesson on spotting good S/R levels in advance, so let's look at this chart moving left to right. First off, we have a very strong bear trend in place, which is evidenced by the strong bearish bars and the complete absence of bullish bars. Notice how the bearish bars increase in size as price dips.

Then the bulls astonishingly pushed back against this force. In what is a sign of the bear strength, despite three strong bullish bars, they run out of steam and price dips back down below. Now, here's the situation. We know that we're in a bearish trend. We also know there's a support level coming up where bulls pushed back against a very strong bear trend. How probable is it that this level will receive bullish support again?

Very probable, one would think. Given that the bearish pressure is nowhere near what it was on the initial dip, odds are that the bulls present at that level will be able to step in again and probably push the price higher this time. This is what happens in mid-September. Indeed, the bulls step in at a higher price level than before. The message to the bears is clear: this is a strongly defended level and it's going to take a lot of firepower to break through.

When price returns to this level in mid-December, it is a strong pushdown but is it as strong as the initial push down? Hardly. So, odds are good that the bulls will hold this level again, and they promptly do. However, the bounce they produce this time around is a lot lower than previously, only three quarters or so of the previous push up. This tells us that the bulls may be weakening.

Bears promptly push price back down and there's no bullish reaction to this push down before price reaching the level. We see that all the bulls can do is hold the price at this level but not push and eventually they exhaust themselves as the bears push through.

What does all this mean for your options strategies? Well, hopefully, it's clear to you what the range boundaries are and what your strike prices for range strategies ought to be. Secondly, as price reaches the support, this is a good time for you to employ some bullish strategies. Do you know when the range bottom will break? Well, maybe but you can't say with any great odds. So a horizontal spread is out.

Instead, any call or put strategy you employ can have its strike prices below the support level, given the inability of price to push past this. You can use the same tactics at the top of the range as well, although the top doesn't give multiple opportunities as the bottom does.

The best opportunity is the push upwards in late November where a clear strike price would be above the resistance boundary. Given the number of hits previously and the way the bears defended this level, the odds are good it will hold. Besides, the overall trend is bearish so perhaps a longer time horizon is warranted. This way, you can capture a greater portion of the time decay in your trade.

Generally speaking, the time you want your counter-trend trades to run should be far lesser than you with trend trades. Is there a fixed template for you to follow? Well, again, it's not that simple. As the range grows older you should expect the odds of it breaking down to increase so you should shorten your time horizon accordingly. The last trade-off, the bottom, for example, would have not run till expiration. Some trial and error, in other words, experience, is needed to nail this.

Keep your risk per trade low at the start and as you gain experience, you'll figure out how long to let your trades run. Even better, hedge your directional option bets with neutral strategies like straddles and strangles or simple strategies like the collar. This way you can earn while you learn.

TIPS

There are some easy to spot characteristics of potentially good S/R levels. I've already mentioned how you need to focus on the order flow characteristics to figure out which levels will be relevant to the current situation. A good place to start is by looking at prior swing points.

Swing points are tricky things to deal with since the level of current order flow imbalance dictates whether the prior swing point will be respected or not. If the order flow at the prior swing point wasn't significant, you can expect an imbalanced current order flow to plummet through it without pause. That was a mouthful to type and understand so we should look at an example of this.

Figure 5: S/R Levels

Figure 5 is the FTSE once more, this time in an uptrend. We can see two swing lows which are indicated by the horizontal lines. The bottom low is more of a zone and is denoted by two horizontal lines. The upper swing low is marked by a single line since the price didn't hang around here for too long before going on upwards.

Now, as price retraces its way back to the original level, how do we determine whether this level will hold or not? Well, we start with the current order flow. Before the first bearish bar into the level, we have the odd scenario of price gapping down on open but still ending up bullish for the day. This is not something you'll see very often and to be honest it can be hard to know what to make of this. Let's reserve judgment for now.

The bearish bar into the level clarifies things immensely though. Not only is it far bigger than the previous bearish bars, but it also comes on the back of bearish pressure previously seen. This is also the biggest bar printed for a long time now. So, we know that order flow is tilted towards the bears. Now, let's look at the potential support which is our upper swing point.

Was the bearish pressure into this level strong? Hardly. Was this a level the bulls had to mount a lot of force into to defend. Given the lackluster bearish attack on it, this doesn't seem to be the case. Thus, we can conclude that this level probably doesn't have much significant bullish presence and we can ignore this level as of the current moment. On a live chart, you need not even mark this level since it is insignificant.

The swing point below is a different matter. While the bearish reaction here was not particularly strong, it was a place where the bears mounted some resistance to pretty steep bullish pressure (look at the angle of the upswing going into the level). Against this sort of bullish pressure, the bears were strong enough to keep the price at this level for quite some time and even dampen the slope of the upswing. The bearish pressure was significant here.

The fact that the bulls overcame this is quite significant. Thus, despite the strong bearish pressure into the lower swing point's level, we can say that the odds of this level holding appear to be good. Do we know for certain that it will hold? No. However, the odds are good and that's all we need. Turns out that in this case, we were correct, but it is possible to be wrong as well, of course, despite the evidence we've seen.

Another key tip for identifying strong S/R levels is to check whether the level is present on a higher time frame. Often, you'll see price form a V top or bottom in a given time frame and this can appear confounding until you go up one level and see that it did this because it bounced off a higher time frame level.

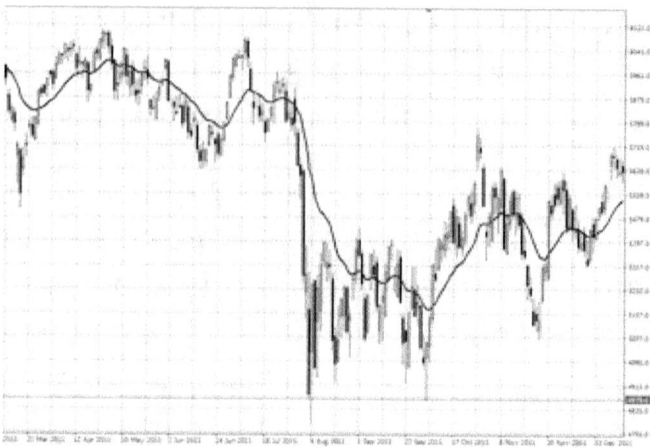

Figure 6: FTSE Daily Bounce

Figure 6 shows a steep downtrend on the FTSE after a range. Initially, this downward swing looks apocalyptic. However, around 4870, price violently bounces back up and the FTSE reverses course as if nothing happened. Not only that, but it also doesn't even approach it again after an initial retest. It's like all that bearish pressure was pointless. What gives?

Well, figure 7 holds the answer. I've marked the level more accurately in this figure and the bounce on the daily is the second bounce on the right-hand side of figure 7. As you can see, the price was headed smack into a very strong level on the weekly chart which had been defended by the bulls previously.

If anything, the current push into the level was mild compared to the previous violent push into this level, as we can see by the tail that is formed on the bearish weekly bar in the first swing point. Seen in this context, the daily bearish push seems rather meek.

If you were aware of this level beforehand, you could have executed a bullish directional strategy with your strike prices beyond the support zone. Odds are with the bearish pressure headed into it; you would have received a good deal on the premiums as well.

Figure 7: FTSE Weekly Bounce

To summarize, here they are:

Prior swing points are good places to start looking for possible S/R.

Prior order flow points where there was significant bullish or bearish pressure are good places to start as well.

Order flow and bias into the level matter. Stronger the imbalance, the stronger the level needs to be to hold price.

Higher time frame S/R points are always significant, irrespective of the lower time frame order flow imbalance. This doesn't mean they'll always hold, just that you can expect the price to hiccup at it at the very least.

Chapter 22
LEARNING HOW TO READ AN OPTIONS CHART

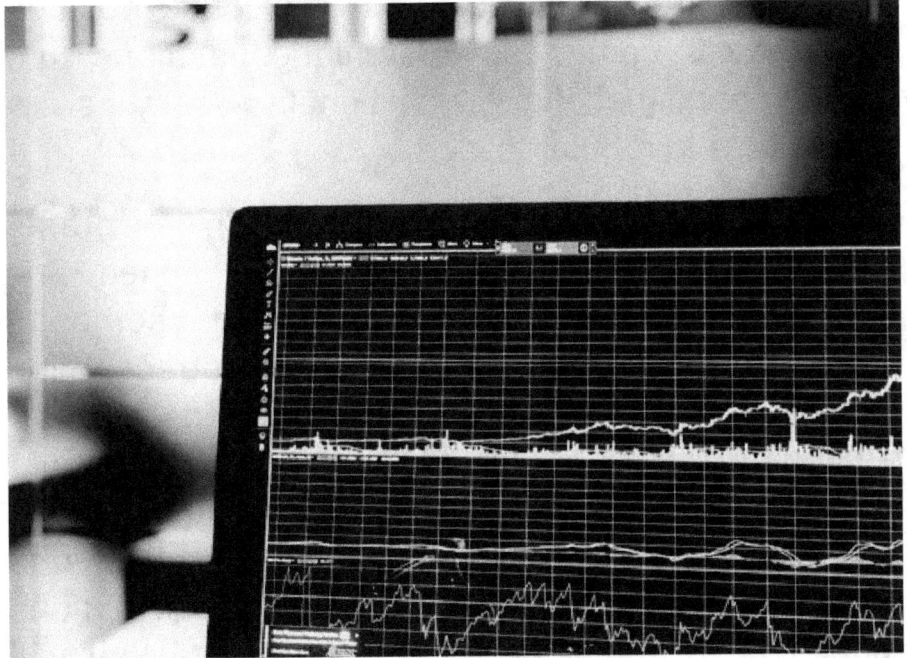

A lot of traders, and investors, have come to learn of the numerous benefits associated with options trading. Many more desire to become wealthy through options trading. This is why the trading volumes at options exchanges have increased steadily over the years.

Data dissemination and electronic trading have enabled more traders and investors to participate in options trading. To create wealth and generate a recurrent income from trading, you must understand the trading process, terminology, and other useful features.

Some investors and traders make use of options to speculate about price direction. Others use them to hedge either an anticipated or existing position while others come up with unique positions that offer irregular benefits. Such benefits are generally unavailable to regular traders.

For instance, as an options trader, you can earn profits should an underlying stock remain unchanged. One of the crucial elements of success when it comes to options trading is learning to select the correct option or even a combination. These are options that are essential for the creation of a position that harbors the appropriate risk-to-reward opportunities. To be successful and create substantial wealth you need to be a savvy trader. What you need to do at the options market is to find sophisticated data sets that will possibly earn you attractive rewards.

PREVIOUS ERA OPTIONS TRADING

Back in the past decade or so, options price reports were sent to newspapers. The newspapers would list a lot of rows of data. Most of the data were illegible and most people could not decipher its meaning. Such data was often printed in the financial sector of the newspapers. Today, however, traders are choosing to search for options data via online sources. Even as each source formats its data differently, the data and variables used are the ones found to be necessary and essential by today's traders.

MODERN DAY OPTIONS TABLE

The table indicated below shows the call options for IBM for March. The table is a computer-generated representation of the said data and is obtained from Optionetics Platinum Software. We will examine the variables listed.

1	2	3	4	5	6	7	8	9	10	11	12
OpSym	Bid (pts)	Ask (pts)	Extrinsic Bid/Ask (pts)	IV Bid/Ask (%)	Delta Bid/Ask (%)	Gamma Bid/Ask (%)	Vega Bid/Ask (pts/% IV)	Theta Bid/Ask (pts/day)	Volume	Open Interest	Strike
IBM MAR10 110 C	16.25	16.70	0.00 0.37	19.77 35.15	99.16 92.06	0.27 1.15	0.007 0.053	0.0009 -0.0279	0	479	110.000
IBM MAR10 115 C	11.65	11.80	0.32 0.47	25.37 27.68	90.52 88.67	1.82 1.90	0.060 0.069	-0.0227 -0.0290	47	552	115.000
IBM MAR10 120 C	7.15	7.30	0.82 0.97	21.85 23.30	79.89 78.51	3.53 3.45	0.101 0.105	-0.0344 -0.0385	360	1179	120.000
IBM MAR10 125 C	3.40	3.50	2.07 2.17	19.04 19.75	58.20 57.98	5.65 5.46	0.141 0.141	-0.0431 -0.0448	1268	5782	125.000
Stock											126.33
IBM MAR10 130 C	1.10	1.14	1.10 1.14	17.41 17.73	28.66 29.04	5.40 5.33	0.123 0.124	-0.0349 -0.0358	1868	3947	130.000
IBM MAR10 135 C	0.23	0.25	0.23 0.25	16.73 17.08	8.45 8.91	2.56 2.61	0.056 0.058	-0.0154 -0.0164	666	6539	135.000
IBM MAR10 140 C	0.04	0.06	0.04 0.06	17.04 18.12	1.82 2.47	0.72 0.88	0.016 0.021	-0.0045 -0.0062	80	4284	140.000
IBM MAR10 145 C	0.00	0.03	0.00 0.03	0.00 21.03	0.00 1.17	0.00 0.40	0.000 0.011	0.0000 -0.0038	10	1747	145.000

If you can learn to read the table above, then you will well be on your way to understanding stock options and increasing your chance of earning big money.

The columns run down while the rows run across. Let us examine the columns closely.

OPSYM

This is found in the first column. The field indicated here represents the underlying stock which in this case is IBM. It also shows the strike price (110,115, 120) the contract month and year and if the option is a call or put. (C or P)

BID (PTS)

The bid price happens to be the price offered specifically by a market maker to purchase a specific option. Therefore, if you place a market order to dispose of the call, then you will dispose of it at the bid price indicated.

ASK (PTS)

The latest price that a market maker introduces to sell an option is known as the asking price. Therefore, when you are trading options at an options exchange, anytime you ask for the market order then you get the asking price.

When you purchase options at the bid price or dispose of options with the asking price, you are providing market makers with an income. It is recommended that a trader should consider the bid and asking price just before trading. The fact is that active options have tighter bids and ask spreads compared to less active ones.

THE EXTRINSIC BID/ASK (PTS)

The quantity of time premium that is injected into the option price is displayed in this column. You need to note that all options ultimately lose their time premium as soon as the option expires. Therefore, the extrinsic bid or ask price indicates the total time value that an option has.

DELTA BID/ASK (%)

Delta is derived from a different pricing model. It represents an option's stock equivalent position. Delta values usually range from zero to 100 for call options while they range from zero to -100 for put options.

GAMMA BID/ASK (%)

Just like Delta, Gamma is a Greek value. This value is similarly derived from yet another option pricing model. It gives you information about the number of deltas that an option stands to lose or gain if the underlying stock goes up by a single point.

VEGA BID/ASK (PTS/% IV)

The Vega value shows the amount of expected rise or fall in the price of an option. This rise and fall would only be based on a single point increase in the stock's volatility. As a trader, you should look to purchase options when the IV or implied volatility is low and then write options when the implied volatility is higher. This way, you will pay a lower time premium.

VOLUME

This column simply indicates the number of contracts that were traded concerning a particular option. Bids and ask spreads are often tighter with large volumes though not all the time.

STRIKE PRICE

In options, the strike price is generally the price at which a buyer of an option gets to pay for its underlying security. Therefore, if a trader wants to exercise their right to purchase the security, the strike price is the price to watch out for.

IMPORTANT POINTS TO KEEP IN MIND

The above information is concerning call options. A put options table would be almost similar to the one above, save for a couple of differences. Here is a look at those differences. You should understand these differences so you know how to apply them.

CALL OPTIONS

Call options are costlier when the strike price is lower. On the other hand, put options are costlier if the strike price is higher. For call options, the options will have the best or highest prices with lower strike prices. This is true also for put options where the prices are low with a higher strike level. The reasons for these circumstances are that every strike price is always either more out-of-the-money or less in-the-money. This is inverse with put options because when the strike prices increase, they become either more in-the-money or less out-of-the-money.

DELTA VALUES

Again, with call options, delta values increase at the low strike price and positive. When it comes to putting options, delta values increase with higher strike prices and are negative. Therefore, when you purchase a put option, you get a negative delta value because it resembles a short position.

MAKE MONEY WITH OPTIONS SPREADING

One of the most common ways of making money with options is through options spreading. This process typically involves the simultaneous purchase and sale of options. This is where the term spreading comes in. Options spreading also refers to the purchase of options combinations. It is important to understand this concept because it is among the most crucial strategies that can earn you plenty of cash repeatedly. Let us examine options spreading closely.

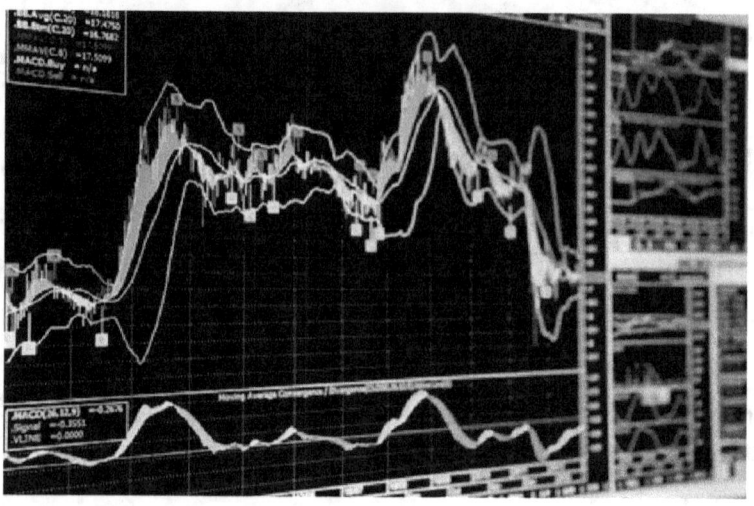

LONG PUTS AND LONG CALLS

Several option positions are commonly used. The simplest of them all is either a long put or a long call on its own.

- You stand to benefit greatly from this position if the underlying asset's price as well as the downside remains limited to the premium.

- A straddle is created when you simultaneously purchase put options that have a similar strike price as well as the expiration date. You will enjoy huge rewards if there is a rise or fall of the underlying asset's price. The only problem is that you get to lose money should the price remain relatively stable.

- We also have a strategy known as strangling. This is a strategy that is employed to purchase a call option and then a put option that has a lower strike. It is this put with a lower strike that gives this strategy its name, strangle. For this strategy to be successful then a large price movement either way is necessary.

- When you are short with either strangle or straddle strategies, you will make good money in a market with minimal movement. Being short simply means that you

OPTIONS SPREAD BUTTERFLIES AND BULLS

There are yet other trading strategies that are crucial for successful traders. These also have great potential and will guide you in making large amounts of money. These will essentially show you how to work with certain spreads. We can have a call or put spread created.

PUT SPREAD

This spread is also known as a bear vertical spread. When dealing with this option type, you will buy a put option then sell another put option that has a lower strike price.

CALL SPREAD

This kind of spread is also known as the bull vertical spread. You can create this spread option if you purchase a call option and at the same time sell a call option that has a larger strike price. You can profit from this kind of trade when there is an increase in the price of the underlying asset.

CALENDAR SPREAD

Anytime that you buy and then sell options that have varying expiration times or dates, then these options are referred to as calendar spreads. It can also be called a time spread.

BUTTERFLIES

We can say that we have a butterfly spread where there exist options at three distinct strikes. These three strikes are equidistant to each other and the options at these points are all of a similar kind. This means they are either all puts or calls and have a similar expiration time.

We can have either a short or long butterfly. Where we have a long butterfly case, you should sell the middle strike option and then purchase the outside strikes. These are often bought at the ratio of 1:2:1. This simply means buy one, sell two and then buy another one. This ratio should hold at all times otherwise the situation will not be a butterfly.

The two outside strikes that we mentioned are regularly referred to as the butterfly's wings while the inside is known as the body. One important factor that you need to keep in mind is that the butterfly's value will never get to zero.

BUTTERFLY SPREAD EXAMPLE

Let us look at an example involving the butterfly spread option. We will go long on a 70 call, then two short at

75 and then go long again with an 80 call option. For our identical trade, we could opt for the two short 75 puts, the long 70 put and 80 put options. Since the butterfly formation is long, it will likely benefit from a market with little activity.

Using the spread example, we can create a synthetic position directly from the options. This kind of strategy is also referred to as the put-call parity. Simply put,

The Call Price − Put Price = Underlying Price − Strike Price

We can use the formula indicated above to come up with a synthetic long call. This is by simply rearranging it. Synthetic puts are simply a combination of a long call and short the underlying security. There are numerous ways of combining all sorts of spreads with trade in the underlying stocks. By doing this, you will be able to achieve many novel positions like the risk reversal, fence, or even collar. These offer you numerous ways of making money.

Chapter 23
TRADING WITH LEAPS

LEAPS ARE INTERESTING OPTIONS

They expire a year or more into the future. This is different from the short-term options that most people are trading. LEAPS are more expensive, but they can also represent money-making opportunities. LEAPS also gives you an indirect way to control stock.

PROFITING FROM LEAPS

LEAPS have high prices because they have a lot of extrinsic value. Looking at June 18, 2021 Facebook call options, the $195 call is priced at $42.13 a share. So that represents a $4,213 options contract. According to the chart, it made 3.4% today, which isn't a huge amount, but I challenge you to find a bank or mutual fund that has a return of 3.4% per day. The open interest is 133. This meets our minimum criteria for getting involved in a trade. It's quite small compared to Facebook options that expire in the next month, but it's enough open interest that it's going to be possible to get in and out of a trade in a reasonable amount of time. The implied volatility is a solid 33%. For comparison, the $195 call that expires in three weeks is priced at $12.48.

Although LEAPS are expensive, they have a lot of potential for profits. You can get into a LEAP and if the stock makes a solid move, you can close your position and make large amounts of money. For that $195 call that expires in June 2021, the delta is 0.64. That means that even though the option has a lot of extrinsic value since it expires a long way into the future, it's pretty sensitive to price changes in the stock that is with the option. If the share price goes up to $1, the option price will go up by $64. LEAPS don't suffer much from time decay. Theta for this option is only 0.03. If the share price goes up to $20 after an earnings call, the option will go up by $1,280. So you can make pretty good profits. The barrier to entry is the high price to buy one.

POOR MAN'S COVERED CALL

One of the interesting things that you can do with a LEAP is you can use it to sell covered calls. That sounds crazy, but it works. You can use the LEAP to cover call options that you sell to open. So you can invest in LEAPS at a fraction of what it costs to invest in the stock, and then start selling calls against the options to generate income. Although it might cost $4,600 to buy a Facebook LEAP, it would cost nearly $20,000 to buy 100 shares of stock. Buying a LEAP gives you de facto control over a hundred shares of stock at a much smaller price than the investment cost.

For the price of 100 shares of Facebook, you could invest in 4-5 LEAPS, and have a lot more room to work with as far as selling call options. So you could end up having a higher income.

Chapter 24
KNOWING YOUR MARKETS

Finally, let's talk about bear and bull markets in options trading. Both are incredibly important to understanding how to utilize options, and here, we'll discuss the market trends, and why they matter, including some tips to help you with this.

THE BEAR MARKET

Bear markets are the first part of this that we will talk about, and it's essentially when there is a general decline in the market over some time. Bear markets will typically swing high investor optimism, to both fear, and pessimism.

There is also a mentality that goes along with this, which is where the market or the stock will drop in value. Bear markets expect it to decline, and from there, sell the commodity at a lower price, which is more speculation in that sort of way. The market typically is more gradually declining, and then will become bullish once again.

Typically, the price of these securities falls about 20% or more from the highest, and usually, the general sentiment is negative. These usually have an association with the declines in an overall market, but usually, the securities are considered on a more individual level if it's a decline of 20% or more over some time, at least 2 months or more. The US major market indexes fell into a bear market level back during the Christmas time of last year. The longest prolonged bear market before that point was between 2007 and 2009, which was during the financial crisis, a time that, if you heard about the housing investment crisis, maybe pretty familiar with it. During that time, it lost about 50% of the value, and investors weren't all that happy with it.

There are different types of bear markets too, and the biggest thing to remember is that these can fall into a much longer prolonged pattern, lasting anywhere from 10-20 years, characterized by a below-average return that happens on a sustainable level. So, if it is a below-average market, but it's a much more prolonged bias on all of this. This also may cause rallies to happen for a long period, since the gains aren't sustained, and the prices revert to the lower levels once again. In contrast, there are cyclical bear markets that last anywhere from a couple of weeks to many years.

Typically, the market will fall to a "market bottom" which is when it gets to the lowest point, signaling the end of the downturn, and the beginning of the upward trend of moving towards a more bullish market.

The problem with this is that while the bottom is reachable, it's very hard to identify what the bottom is, while this is happening. The same can go with a bullish market and the upturn, which we will get to in a minute.

But, the problem is, if you fall into the trap of assuming that the market bottom is at one point, and it turns out to be "false" it actually can cause you to lose profit trying this since you're selling it for lower prices than what you care to utilize.

Now, let's talk about a bull market, and from there, discuss how you can look into potentially predicting these trends.

BULL MARKETS

In complete contrast, you have the bull market, which is the market where the securities are rising, and they expect to rise. This is often used in the stock market but can be used for bonds, real estate, currencies, and other commodities. Because the prices of these essentially rise and fall during this, bull markets are essentially the trend of the prices for this rising, and they can last months, or in some cases years as well.

Bull markets are characterized by confidence, optimism, and the expectations that stronger results should continue for an extended period. It's difficult to predict it with the trends in the market, and part of the difficulty is the psychology of the speculation, and how it plays a part in this. There isn't a specific metric that identifies a bull market, unfortunately, but one of the most common characteristics is that the stock prices rise at least 20%, with it following after a drop of 20%, so typically the market goes into a bear form before it becomes bull. Since bull markets are hard to predict, usually, this happens. The most notable bull market is between 2003-2007, which is right after a decline, but then, after a bit, the 2008 financial crisis hit, and from there, it hit the market with major declines, but again, this was right after a bull market happened. So, it goes bear, then bull, and then bear once more, following this pattern appropriately.

Bull markets tend to happen when the economy is strong, or it's already growing strong, and it happens when the GDP and the unemployment rates are good, and there is a rise in profits on a corporate level, with more demand for stocks generally. It helps with the overall tone of the market too, and it increases the IPO activity during this time. It also is much more quantifiable in measurement than others. Some of the other factors in this are hard to quantify though since supply and demand do still seesaw in this case. Many are eager to get securities, and investors are more than willing to get rid of their stock to gain profits. There is much more happening with how the market goes around, and the transactions are done, and many people are trading during this point.

Essentially, these do coincide with the economic cycle, which goes through phases of expansion, peaking, contraction, and then the trough, which is the lowest point. It involves a lot more economic expansion, since public sentiment about the economic conditions does drive the stock a little bit, and the prices tend to rise much higher than they did before. Bear markets usually happen right before a contraction economically happens, such as the recession happening right before a large and expanding stock market.

TRADING IN BEAR MARKETS

So to profit in bear markets, investors do look at taking short positions or short selling, which is when you borrow and anticipate it to fall once again. This, in turn, will allow you to cover a position that you're profiting from. You can from there buy back the shares to close it out, profiting from the fall. Short positions are extremely risky though, with unlimited potential losses. I would recommend against shorting stocks in a bear market.

Put options are your best friend, and essentially that is because you're giving the right to sell something at a strike price in the future. The money you pay is a premium, and put options increase when the stock falls, so it makes sense to use this in a bear market. If it falls below the strike price, you can then sell it at a higher price, or sell it completely for profit.

You should also consider short ETFs, which is essentially the returns that are inverse of the index. If you decide to trade a stock that performs inverse on Nasdaq 100, about 25%, it will then later on rise above 25%, and rise itself proportionally. The inverse relationship is good for those who want to profit when the market is downturned, or who want to hedge the long positions against this, in turn making sure that they get a profit.

You want to trade with the idea of profiting in a falling market.

TRADING IN BULL MARKETS

If you want to benefit from a bull market, you need to buy early to take advantage of their rising prices, and from there wait to sell them when they reach the peak price. However, it is hard to determine how to go about this, but there are a few ways to do this.

First and foremost, you want to consider going along with your positions. Wait a bit, and you can always buy and hold, which is buying security, holding onto it, and then selling it later on. This brings about more confidence for the investor, and it will allow you to look at market trends, and then trade and sell when the time is right.

Also, consider getting a long position, since it will let you profit the longer it's happening. You also want to exercise call options, since that gives you the right to buy the stock at the time. Calls go up when the value of the stock rises. If the stock rises past the strike price, the person can buy it, but you can still consider writing these, and continue to write these and make a profit since you can keep the stock above the strike price, and let it continue that.

Finally, you want to consider long ETFs, which allow you to have low transaction costs and operating expenses. They replicate the movement of the indexes followed, fewer expenses. For example, if the stock rises by 10%, the ETF then will rise by the same amount.

Finally, you want to consider retracement additions, which is a period in which the trend in the security is reversed, and even during bull markets, it's unlikely that it will only ascend. You want to look for retracements within this, and presume that if the market does continue, it will move up, and provide the investor with a discounted price.

HOW TO SPOT THESE MARKETS

The truth is, it's very hard to predict these, and some believe that predicting these is the key to investing, but it isn't that easy for you to do. Many will sell in bear markets since they don't want to risk the bigger losses at this point.

Now, the advance/decline line essentially shows the number where the stocks are advancing, or declining. If you see that it's exceeding the declines, it definitely will have a positive number to it. If you notice that the declines are exceeding the advances, it's a declining line. This shows the number of times when a stock is falling.

If the number is greater than 1, it's advancing, but if it's less, it's declining, and traders can use this to plot the performance of a stock, and also compare it with the overall performance of a stock. If you see divergences, whether bearish or bullish, this is a chance that it might have a reversal and is a sign of it.

If it's been declining for a few months, but the averages are higher than usual, this is a negative correlation, and that usually means that a bear market is happening. The advance/decline line that continues to move down shows that the averages are weak, but if it rises again for a few months, and then the averages are moved down, it creates a positive divergence, which means that bull markets are starting to form, so it may be in your best interest to potentially trade in that market.

This is probably your best tool since it helps with determining trends and making it work.

If you notice that investors are acting fearful and pessimistic during bear markets, a lot of times they'll fall into the trend of "panic selling" which is when they sell their shares in a panic. But, if you notice that there is more happening during a bull market, it involves more liquidity, higher trading volumes, and further raising of the stock prices.

The best way to look at this, and to trade in each market is to look at the different advance/decline lines, look at the cycle, and from there, keep an incredibly diverse portfolio. Maintain enough liquidity to ride out the hard periods, so you don't have to resort to panic selling. Following this can help you prevent the worst from happening, and it can work to prevent this from getting worse over time, and in turn, make it easier for you to sell as well.

Chapter 25
BASIC OPTIONS STRATEGIES: GOING LONG

If you were to first open your contract by selling, we say that you are "short". If you buy to open a position, we say that you are "long". The simplest way to trade options is to take a long position on a call or a put. Although when buying and selling stocks we say that someone "shorts" the stock when they are hoping to profit off a decline in share price, you can be hoping to profit from a decline in share price, but you are "long" concerning the put option.

The strategy for profiting from going long on a call or put option is simple. You are hoping the price of the stock would move in your favor so that you will earn a profit. The industry is full of naysayers that downplay this basic strategy; however, the reality is you can earn profits in this way. That is buying or selling individual options, be they the call or put variety. The key to success when doing this type of trading is to stay on top of it and don't buy options on a whim. You need a good reason to buy a call or a put option by itself, and that means paying attention to the financial news surrounding the company, earnings reports, and looking at simple market trends to determine when you have a reasonable probability of earning a profit.

DAY TRADING AND OPTIONS

This is just an aside but watching the movement of a stock price over a single day can provide opportunities to ride a short-term trend in price and profit handsomely. Rising and falling share prices are magnified in the price of the option, so when the share price goes up a few tens of cents, you might profit by $65 or $75 in a single day.

But be aware that the rules for day trading apply to options as well. To be a day trader approved by your broker in the United States, you need to have a margin account and it needs to have $25,000 deposited in the account. Since options trading often takes place on the level of tens or hundreds of dollars at a time, the vast majority of beginning options traders won't be looking to be a day trader. But you are tempted to get out of some trades on the same day that you enter the trade because you might have ridden a trend in one direction or the other to significant profits. The trend might not continue the following day, and you don't want to eat some of your profits from the theta or time decay.

The rule you need to be aware of is if you make four-day trades over five days, that means you will be labeled a pattern day trader. To keep your account open, you'd have to fund it with $25,000. So, this is a situation that you are probably going to want to avoid. To avoid being pulled under by this, simply limit the number of day trades to 3 per week.

Remember that the five-day rule means five consecutive trading days, so weekends don't count. If you made a day trade on Friday, the following Monday, that day trade still counts against you.

CALL OPTIONS BASIC STRATEGY

The basic strategy behind making profits with call options is to buy low and sell high. You can profit from this strategy riding a single day's price movements or by "swing trading" the option over one or more days, meaning that you will hold the option overnight. You won't hold the option until expiration unless you have the intention of buying the stock.

The time to sell the option is the point at which you have made an acceptable level of profits. You should set this level beforehand so that you are not letting the emotions of the moment rule your decisions. It's not uncommon to make $50 or $100 profits in a few days or even in a single day off of one option contract, but many traders get dollar signs in their eyes – they get overcome with greed – and as a result, they hold their positions too long. That can mean lost profits, defeat by time decay, or even seeing the option wiped out.

One lesson that you will learn is that options prices can fluctuate dramatically. This is because the underlying stock is 100 shares. So a small change in the stock price is magnified by 100 for your investment in the option. Using a one-to-one pricing relationship for the sake of simplicity, if the price of the stock moves up by a mere 45 cents, the price of the option will go up by $45. On the other hand, if it drops by 30 cents, the price of the option would drop $30.

The key to success with trading options is to have a trading plan that you follow, and which has specific rules. We will cover that at the end of the chapter.

One skill you will need to develop when it comes to calling options is the ability to read stock charts. The details of this are beyond the scope of this book, you can learn about it online or purchase a book on day trading. There are three basic skills that I recommend you have:

Learn how to read and interpret candlestick charts.

Learn how to use moving averages.

Learn how to use and interpret Bollinger bands.

Let's briefly discuss each of these in turn. A candlestick chart divides a stock chart into time intervals that you specify. The time interval you will use will depend on the time frame over which you are hoping to trade. I have had some success trading call options using a buy to open strategy. I can't say what the situation is in all cases, but what I will tell you is that I don't stay in these trades very long. What I do is I check the early morning financial news for any surprises, and then when the market opens, I look for early indicators of how it's going to move.

If the other aspects of the stock look good – that is I can buy options with a high level of open interest – then I will enter a position if it looks like there will be a strong move over the day or the next few days.

Let's give a few specific examples so that you will have some practical advice for the situation. You can trade index funds like the Dow Jones Industrial Average (trade options on DIA), the S & P 500 (trade options on SPY), or the NASDAQ (trade options on QQQ). These index funds are very sensitive to general economic and political news. So, if you see that a good jobs report has come out, that is a good signal to get in on one or more of these funds. It's often worth the risk to get in on options for these index funds the day before. Then you can wake up and see the results. It's going to be possible to double an investment overnight. Since you are not day trading, in that case, it's a simple matter to exit your positions for a profit. But keep in mind, there is a risk as well if it works against you (we will discuss strategies to use to cover both movements). If you buy a call but the early indication is a market sell-off, then get rid of the put first thing when the market opens.

This is a good example of why open interest is important to look at. If you were to buy an option on something with a small level of open interest, you might not be able to get rid of your options before the put lost a lot of money. With something that is very heavily traded like SPY, however, it's a sure bet that you can unload the put quickly.

You also want to pay attention to news about specific companies. For example, if there is news coming out in the early morning hours that the government will investigate the social media companies, that is a good indication that going long on a put option would be a reasonable strategy. Conversely, recently, the FTC announced a settlement with Facebook, and this sent the stock soaring.

You won't be getting the news "first" as an individual retail investor, but the good news is that with options trading if you are staying on top of things, you are able to get in and out of your trades and take profits if you are careful about it.

READING THE CHARTS

As an options trader, you will have to learn how to read charts. The first thing to do is look up candlestick patterns so that you can recognize when a trend reversal might be coming. Candlestick patterns are not absolute rules or truth-tellers, they are an indicator. So you consider the candlestick charts and use the entirety of the information that you have available to make your decisions.

As we said earlier, a candlestick can be divided into different timeframes. If you are looking to ride a trend over a single day, a five-minute time frame is good to use. In this case, each candlestick will tell you what the price action was over five minutes.

The candlesticks are colored green or red. If a candlestick is green, it's a "bullish" candlestick. That means that throughout interest, the closing price had risen to a larger higher than the opening price. By itself, it does not tell you where the price is headed. For a bullish candlestick, the top of the candle is the price at the end of the trading session, and the bottom of the body is the price at the start.

Each candlestick has "wicks" that come out of the top and bottom of the candlestick. The top wick gives you a high price for the time interval. The bottom candlestick gives you the low price of the time interval.

If a candlestick is red, that is a "bearish" candlestick. In that case, this means that the closing price was lower than the opening price. So, the top of the body is the opening price in this case, and the bottom of the body is the closing price (the price closed lower than it opened at). The meaning of wicks is the same.

A complete investigation of candlesticks is beyond the scope of this book, so please see online resources or books specifically addressing the topic, or day trading, to learn the patterns that you need to be looking for.

That said, here are the general rules for entering and exiting trades.

In the event of big news that you know will cause a massive move in the share price, you want to just get in early in the trading day.

If you are looking at a stock under normal conditions, that is no earnings report, or other huge news, you want to wait for a downtrend in the share price so that you can enter a position at a relative minimum. So, you buy the option at the lowest possible price given current market conditions. Then you wait until the price rises and the trend peaks out, and you close your position.

For beginners, I have to say get ready for the ride. If you are thin-skinned, this kind of trading will put you on pins and needles. As you know, stock prices do not follow a steady curve, they move up and down a lot. And as we have mentioned several times, a small move in share price which isn't all that significant can have a big impact on options prices. It's not uncommon to get into a trade and see your option lose $75 or $100 for a couple of hours, and then see it rise to a $50 or $100 profit a few hours later. So, this is not something for the faint of heart to get involved with.

But to avoid panic, you should rely on the indicators to help you make your decisions rather than relying on emotion.

The second big tool you need to use in your trading is the moving average. I like to use a 9-period case. This will be for an exponential moving average. Then for the long one, I will use twenty periods. Again, it will be an exponential moving average on the same chart. Moving averages average out the stock prices to give you smooth curves that show the overall price trend. Using two moving averages allows you to get signals when a trend will reverse. This works quite well in practice. The signal for a reversal is when the moving averages cross.

If a short period moving average crosses above a long period moving average, this is taken to be a signal of a coming uptrend.

If the short period moving average crosses below the long period moving average, that means that a downward trend is coming. So, if you have been riding a trend with a call option, that might be an indicator to sell to close your position.

You can also add a tool called the RSI to your charts, which is the relative strength indicator. This tells you if a stock is overbought or oversold. If the RSI is 70 or above, then the stock is considered to be overbought, and that can be a good time to exit a long call position. If the RSI is 30 or below, this is "oversold", and so it can be a good time to enter a long position for call options. I take the RSI with a grain of salt because I've seen it indicate overbought conditions which were then followed by continually rising prices, all too often. But it's one thing that you can consider looking at.

Finally, there are the Bollinger bands. These give you a moving average along with the standard deviation both above and below the moving average. If you will use this, the main reason would be to establish levels of support and resistance. A level of support is a low-price level that the stock is unlikely to break below over a short period. A level of resistance is the maximum price you are likely to see for the stock over a short period. These are guidelines, a stock might suddenly break out of a range at any time.

Another reason to use Bollinger bands is for a guideline when selling to open a position. In this case, you could use one or two standard deviations to give you a boundary above and below which it's extremely unlikely the stock price will move. We will talk more about that later.

PUT OPTION STRATEGY

The strategy for put options is a little bit different than what most people are used to thinking of. In this case, if you take a long position with a put option, you are expecting the market value of the shares to drop. The cost of the shares must drop below the strike price of the put for it to be in the money. You will use the same tools that you would use to analyze stock charts that you will use when going long on calls. The only difference is that you will enter and exit your positions in the opposite manner. So, a petering out uptrend is the time to enter into a position by buying a put option. Then when a downtrend seems to be running out of steam, you would close your position by selling the put option. Put options can be a consideration just as much as call options, but beginning traders tend to be wedded to the commonsense approach that you profit when the stock price rises. If you will enter into this kind of activity, you want to rid yourself of that notion and be ready to profit no matter which way the share price is moving. This will massively expand the opportunities you have available even if you just stick to buying and trading calls and put options without using any advanced strategies.

CAN YOU PROFIT WITH THE MONEY OR OUT OF THE MONEY OPTIONS?

The short answer is yes. Out of the money, options have a lot of appeals because they are cheap, relatively speaking. They also get a large percentage of movements from share prices when there is a dramatic move over a short time frame. For comparison, I am looking at some SPY options. The S & P 500 went up the day that I am writing this and is priced at $299.70 a share. The more in the money the option, the smaller its gains. Although when you see the gains and compare them to the kinds of gains you would get from any other financial investment, they are massive. And in the money, a $299 call rose in value by 84.76%. The $299.50 call went up by 94.6%.

Now, look at the out of the money options. The $300 call is slightly out of the money, and it went up in value by 104.69%. The $301 call went up by 118.1%.

So, people that tell you that you shouldn't trade out of the money options don't know what they are talking about. You can profit from trading out of the money options. If you can buy an option for $40, and it goes up 100% so you could sell it for $80, isn't that a good deal? Imagine if you had traded 10 of them, that would be a $400 profit.

The $300 call has a theta of -0.126. It's currently trading at $1.31, for a total of $131. That means at market open the price will drop by almost $13 to $118. But if you had purchased it in the morning before it had made the 104% gain, you can still sell it the following day for a big profit – and if the share price keeps rising the next day, that means that it may make even more significant profits the following day that will overcome the $13 lost to time decay, and possibly drive your profits much higher.

You can also trade out of the money put options, but the time to buy out of the money options is when the stock is making a significant move one way or the other. As we'll see, out of the money options also have important roles to play in many advanced options strategies.

The only caution I would offer here is don't go too far out of the money. You can buy a $310 call on SPY for just $1, but it declined in value by 50%.

HAVING A TRADING PLAN

Having a trading plan in place will be important no matter what you do in the stock market. A trading plan should include the following:

YOUR OVERALL GOAL

This can include your reasons for investing as well as your goal for annual profits or ROI (return on investment).

HOW MUCH YOU ARE WILLING TO PUT AT RISK

It should go without saying that you shouldn't bet the family farm on your trades. Set aside a fixed amount of money that you are willing to lose. If you are smart about your trading, you are unlikely to lose all of it, and hopefully, you don't have a string of losing trades. With options, you can start small and learn the ropes without risking large amounts of money. So start with something like $500. If you lose $500, it won't be the end of the world. If that happens, you can replenish it later, and it probably won't put you in a position where you can't eat.

HAVE A TAKE PROFIT LEVEL FOR THE TRADE

This is done on a per-contract basis. The level I like to use is $50. You are indeed going to miss out on some big gains some of the time, but having a fixed level ensures that overall you have a string of profitable trades. Remember that it is per contract, so you can trade five contracts on the same option and if you reach the $50 profit level, that is $250 in overall profit.

HAVE AN EXIT STRATEGY

This is a personal tolerance level of risk. For me, it's a $100 loss on one contract, provided there are no signs of a turnaround coming. This is harder to quantify because options move up and down by large amounts over short periods. So, if you are not somewhat flexible, getting out on a price move that is too small will cause you to lose out on a lot of trades. Remember that a $100 loss on a trade is only a price movement of $1-$2 on the underlying stock. A stock that drops by $1 is just as likely to reverse course and go up by $1.

ALWAYS WATCH TIME DECAY

You can profit on options at any time, but if you buy an option that you intend to hold for several days, potential losses from time decay must be taken into account. One mistake that beginners make is not paying attention to time decay.

NEVER LET OPTIONS EXPIRE

Another beginner's mistake is to buy options and just hold onto them waiting to see what's going to happen. Never hold onto an out of the money option. Even if you will sell it for a large loss, get out of it if the expiration date is approaching. When it comes to the money options, you might sell the day before expiration. You probably won't want to keep an in the money option past that unless you want it exercised.

Chapter 26
BEST WAYS TO IMPROVE YOUR OPTIONS TRADING EDUCATION

There are a few different ways to expand your options trading training. The vast majority of them permanently require your time and may not cost any cash forthright. While there are a lot of different techniques for finding out about options trading, here are three ordinarily utilized chances.

COACH

Starting an association with an options broker as your tutor is likely the ideal approach to learn. There is nothing superior to anything utilizing genuine models as a significant aspect of your options trading instruction. Books, distributions, and other hard copy materials can offer excellent material - however, nothing looks at first-hand involvement. Having a tutor will give you an unmistakable preferred standpoint over your opposition.

MIMICKED TRADES

If you have a record with an online intermediary, at that point you may now put reenacted options exchanges. This can be an incredible learning instrument for those hoping to build their options trading instruction. Purchasing and selling options through mimicked exchanges is first-hand knowledge of how the general financial exchange functions, without the danger of losing real cash.

BOOKS AND PUBLICATIONS

While not the cheapest option, utilizing magazines or different productions to expand your online options training works very well for certain financial specialists. You may likewise hope to agree to accept part sites or expect minimal effort eBooks to facilitate your instruction. Do whatever it takes not to spend a great deal of cash on these as you can most likely discover a ton of free data too.

Regardless of whether you are finding out about selling secured calls, purchasing and selling somewhere down in the cash calls, or finding out about investment opportunity sites - instructing yourself is a significant advance in turning into a fruitful dealer.

TRADING EDUCATION IS THE KEY

Likewise, with anything throughout everyday life, training is vital for progress. If you know, at that point you can do anything you set your brain to. This incorporates online options trading just as turning into a savvy speculator of the financial exchange. If you are fueled with the correct data and can gain from your oversights, there is no determining what sort of financial specialist you can be!

For extra data on Options Trading appeal, look at:

OPTIONS INCOME SYSTEM FOR MORE SUBTLETIES.

Adapt precisely how to make a month to month pay, rake in huge profits in the market whether it goes up or down, day exchange with certainty and significantly more...

FINANCIAL DERIVATIVES - WHY TRADING SIMULATORS ARE THE FASTEST AND BEST WAY TO LEARN

There are not many, in any, pragmatic aptitudes that are procured by hypothetical learning alone. Trading financial derivatives are, in such manner, unquestionably not an exemption to the standard. But when the vast majority who are new to derivatives, regardless of whether they are student traders in speculation banks or private people, first methodology trading such items, they submerge themselves in books about the hypothesis, arithmetic, and demonstrating.

In endeavoring to secure different abilities, no less specialized, practice is given need over hypothesis in pretty much every case. In the case of learning to play the violin or how to direct relevant examinations, any art is best learned by doing. Unquestionably, the hypothesis has its place. Without some primary direction, what other site does somebody start? It is each of the issues of equalization. Furthermore, as for learning how to trade financial derivatives, typically things are out of kilter. As of not long ago, it has all been hypotheses, and next to no training.

So why has this been the situation? There is a particular reason why people new to financial derivatives, regardless of whether they intend to trade, oversee hazard, or need to comprehend them for expert purposes, give the excessive load to hypothesis overtraining. Also, that is the trouble in finding a reasonable preparation condition. The financial markets themselves are probably going to make for expensive teachers. Given the hazardous idea of derivatives, missteps can be costly. However, when learning any new expertise, it is through the very demonstration of committing errors that one learns and, from that point, improves. In the case of learning how to drive or how to explain complicated conditions, committing mistakes along the way is an essential piece of the learning procedure.

With regards to financial derivatives, this way has up to this point not been available. Since derivatives are, by their tendency, more convoluted than straightforward stocks and offers, the chance to work on trading in a reproduced domain has not existed until in all respects as of late. Luckily, this circumstance is presently changing, and another age of online derivatives trading simulator is developing. These offer clients the chance to learn how derivatives work through realistic practice sessions, intelligent assistance systems, and point by point investigation of the client's presentation. Furthermore, instead of just focusing on the essential, directional properties of derivatives, the new advances teach clients how financial derivatives work in full. This enables clients to encounter derivatives trading, with all the related dangers and openings, in a totally chance free condition., before they adventure into the live markets.

Such innovation is the front line. It offers critical focal points over the old methods for learning how derivatives work and trade, and for anybody either planning to ace derivatives trading or merely searching for an underlying knowledge, it gives a vital learning device.

DEPENDABLE GUIDELINE: THE DO'S AND DON'TS OF OPTIONS TRADING

There are many dependable guidelines to pursue as a starting trader, and this part will break down a portion of the do's and don'ts of options trading.

Try not to assess the situation and option trading tips. Mainly as a beginner trader, once people comprehend what you accomplish professionally, you'll likely get a wide range of stock and option trading tips from companions, family, colleagues, maybe even outsiders who just met you. A tipster will prescribe a stock dependent on some "insider data" concerning an organization or a commodity, however trading dependent on stock tips can devastate your record.

Without incorporating some trading procedures in their proposal, the tipster could be setting you up for disappointment. Tuning in to tips is OK, yet regardless you have to play out your own very prepared, exceedingly talented due persistence for any stock or options trade. You have to answer the "who, what, where, when, and why" of that trade.

Along with these similar rules of due persistence, here's another tip: never get into a trade except if you realize the amount, you're willing to lose versus what you hope to make.

Do deal with your money well. You need to ensure that you are rehearsing legitimate money for the executive's abilities. Ensure that before you put a trade on, you have built up a familiar object. Notwithstanding the tremendousness or vacancy of your wealth and the rule measure of money you're contributing, never sink over 10% of your portfolio in one trade, one stock, one option, or one division.

One rule to pursue is the standard of ten. Put 10% of each trade you make into one stock or options and attempt to have 8-10 positions on the double. That way, in case you're in ten distinct areas, and one loses money in your record, it's easy for you to dump and you're not leaving the business.

Also, that raises another "do." You need to treat your trading vocation as a business. If you have ten workers, and you have one terrible seed, you must cut the string. The equivalent goes for trading. You must dispose of that trade that is costing you money and assets and discover a substitution.

Do work on trading with a phony record before you dispatch a real existence, money subsidized trading, or broker record. There are many excellent trading simulators available, many of them through whatever broker you choose to trade with. There are likewise a lot of programming organizations out there that have great phony trading stages available for buy and download. You can rehearse, similarly as though you're trading real money, consistently until you become active and agreeable in your new trading skin.

When you can't profit in a trading test system, at that point you're tricking yourself if you believe you will benefit in a subsidized, live trading record.

Make trade money that you can bear to lose, and don't contact any cash you can't. Try not to utilize the $10,000 charge card limit you're endorsed to take out a $5,000 loan credit to subsidize your trading business. You can't bear to lose that money. What's "reasonable" is diverse for everybody, so you need to take a cold, hard item to take a gander at your startup capital you plan to distribute to your trading business. Be sincerely and financially arranged to lose everything - because it can occur.

You've settled on a great decision in choosing that trading for dynamic and automated revenue is the right business move for you, and stocks, options, and other open, open financial markets are an excellent method to arrive. With Invest to Success' 10 Steps to Trading Success, you will learn how to position yourself to make every day, week after week reliably, and monthly profits for your portfolio with insignificant hazard, regardless of whether you're pristine to trading or a seasoned star!

HOW TO BECOME A TOP OPTIONS TRADING EXPERT

Trading investment opportunities, when contrasted and regular stock trading, has numerous points of interest. Much the same as different sorts of contributing, it is fundamentally essential to have an adequate measure of information about the kind of speculations before setting out on this endeavor.

Online Stock Options trading has turned out to be a standout amongst the best ventures which have exploited the increasing velocity and accessibility of the web. The sheer volume of online trade has abandoned conventional brokers, the sheer volume of online business has left regular brokers, and options trading has turned out to be accessible to an extensive global network, who presently take an interest in the broad US market quickly.

If you have next to no learning about investment opportunities, it is fundamental that you do your research before beginning. Read a book or go to classes. Investment opportunities have different kinds of trading, buying and selling accessible and can in this manner be entangled. Make sure of the types of options you need to attempt and research the particular area. Realize the trading terms; a large number of which are recorded underneath.

Calls

Puts

Long and short call

Long and short put

Long and short engineered

Get back to and set back spread

Call-bull and put-bull spread

Secured call

Defensive put

Neckline

Call-bear and put-bear spread

A long and short straddle

Short and Long guts

Put-time and Call-time spread.

Call-proportion and put-apportion vertical

Short-call and Long-call butterfly

Long-put and short-put butterfly

Long and short condor

Know at any rate the essential meanings of these terms.

Make certain to make sure to use the broad assets accessible on the web and buy into the different bulletins for investment opportunities trading. Become an individual from gatherings and be present on options trading news. Make it your propensity to every day read what's happening in the market.

A decent method to begin your raid into trading is to try out a course, system, or use instructional exercises. Many free instructional practices are offered online that will give you the fundamentals of investment opportunities and trading. A portion of these instructional exercises have recordings, precedents, and other intuitive materials which will demonstrate value to new to trading investment opportunities. An assortment of on the web and disconnected courses are likewise accessible and may incorporate eBooks, gatherings, participation, spreadsheets, recordings, sound documents, DVDs, and different materials. Courses uniquely intended to train you on the most proficient method to trade can be precious to option trading novice.

In conclusion, there are various programming systems and bundles for options trading that can assist you with analyzing and mimic situations in options trading and can be essential devices in your investment opportunities trading.

Chapter 27
TRADING SIGNALS AND TRADING SIGNAL PROVIDERS

FLAG

This first example of a trading signal is relatively simple to understand. A flag symbol is rectangular, very short, and usually slants in the opposite direction of the market trend. It represents a brief moment when the market breathes and remains relatively neutral before continuing the trend it had been going on previous to the flag.

This moment of calm before continuing the trend is called the consolidation period. After spotting the flag on a bullish continuation pattern, investors may decide to begin buying calls, since the trade price is low, and investors expect it to rise following the trend. Spot a flag on a trendline by looking for wherever two parallel lines perfectly frame the visual market trend.

PENNANT

This chart is a short-term chart continuation pattern. With a pennant pattern, a symmetrical triangle points its peak at the market pattern increase or decrease, depending on whether the pattern is bullish or bearish, respectively. In general, a pennant is formed just after a flag symbol, and consequently, it is sometimes referred to as a flag pennant. Since the goal of a trading signal is to predict when it is a good time to buy or sell, using a bullish or bearish pennant pattern to predict market trends can further inform which strategies to use to maintain or appreciate assets.

RECTANGLE

The rectangle trade signals are very similar to a flag with one exception: unlike the flag, the rectangle signal has a much longer and more resistant consolidation period. This essentially means that during the consolidation period, investors may have a hesitant attitude towards the market. The trend will measure the mindset of participants (a.k.a. willingness to sell and buy), which results in a regular horizontal pattern tightly compacted between the sharp market trends.

When looking at a trendline, investors will easily be able to see where long rectangle boxes are in the lines and will use it to make market predictions.

TRIANGLE

There are three types of triangle patterns: ascending, descending, and symmetrical. These correlate to a neutral, bearish, and bullish pattern, respectively. According to writers Chad Langager and Casey Murphy at Investopedia, "The basic construct of this chart pattern is the convergence of two trendlines-flat, ascending or descending-with the price of the security moving between the two trendlines" (Langager, Murphy, Analyzing Chart Patterns). Depending on the nature of the trendline, as well as the resistance and support (meaning whether investors feel the trading price will move down or up) occurring within the triangle, investors may choose to hold long or short positions upon the breakout, which is when the trendline abandons the triangle pattern.

WEDGE

Wedges fall into two categories: rising and falling. These can then make an appearance in a bullish or bearish pattern. The tricky aspect of the wedge is that for a novice, it will look like the market price will continue to rise at first glance. However, once the trendline breaks out of the wedge, it will move in the opposite direction as when it was in the wedge. This means that investors, generally speaking, upon spotting a wedge, know that the market will start moving in the other direction. That is the moment many investors will begin initiating new strategies to take advantage of the market change.

HEAD-AND-SHOULDER

This signal is used to determine when a trend will become exhausted and reverse itself. It depicts a clear balance within the market as sellers bring the trendline down and buyers push it back up again. This signal can be indicative of an upward or downward trend, depending upon the current market climate. Generally, the market will rally three times; after the last shoulder (or third peak) the trend will reverse its bullish or bearish position. Like other signals, investors can use this information to buy or sell calls and puts as necessary.

Some beginning investors who are intimidated by trade indicators elect to become members of online signal providers whom investors can pay to be alerted of any potentially major shifts in the market, which an investor can then use to his or her advantage. Unfortunately, as the saying goes, nothing in this world comes for free. Trade signal providers can cost a hefty amount of money, since the best trade signal providers take risk management into account and offer clients an array of packages that will sort each individual's needs in terms of trade interests, investments, and starting capital.

However, investors should always be wary when signing up for services from signal providers. The

Internet is littered with scams and more often than not, a supposedly trusted signal provider pops up as false mere months after being touted as one of the best signal providers available. A clear warning sign that an investor is stepping into a scam is when a provider offers services free of charge. Additionally, fraudulent sites will require the trader to invest a certain amount of capital, which the trader is then sure to lose. Even if the investor believes he or she has found a secure site, in-depth research must be conducted before buying a membership to any signal provider site.

Chapter 28
MARKET ENVIRONMENT

At this point, you have all the strategies to trade options for all kinds of market conditions, be it neutral, bearish, or bullish. While the strategies by themselves will limit your risk and give you rewards according to their risk profiles, the biggest risk in all of these is you applying the wrong strategy to the wrong market conditions.

No strategy can eliminate the risk of you making a mistake, unfortunately. Even a neutral strategy, like the straddle or strangle, will not work if you misread a range for a trend.

Technical and fundamental analysis will help you determine what market conditions are appropriate. While every trader has different perspectives on this, I tend to lean more towards technical analysis when it comes to determining which stocks to operate in. This is because fundamental analysis favors longer timelines, of over 5 years, for investment purposes. While the earnings announcements are important, a fundamentally low valuation doesn't play itself out for a few months.

Thus, I'll be focusing mostly on technical analysis methods from here on out. Before we get to all of that though, you need to understand some basics about the market environment: namely, what is a trend and what is a range.

TRENDS AND RANGES

A market is a chaotic place with several traders vying for dominance over one another. There are a countless number of strategies and time frames in play and at any point, it is close to impossible to determine who will emerge with the upper hand. In such an environment, how is it then possible to make any money? After all, if everything is unpredictable, how can you get your picks right?

Well, this is where thinking in terms of probabilities comes into play. While you cannot get every single bet right, as long as you get enough right and make enough money on those to offset your losses, you will make money in the long run. This goes back to what I spoke about in the risk management chapter.

It's not about getting one or two right. It's about executing the strategy with the best odds of winning over and over again and ensuring that your math works out with regards to the relationship between your win rate and average win.

So, it comes down to finding patterns which repeat themselves over time in the markets. What causes these patterns? Well, the other traders of course! To put it more accurately, the orders that the other traders place in the market are what create patterns that repeat themselves over time.

The first step to understanding these patterns is to understand what trends and ranges are. Identifying them and learning to spot when they transition into one another will give you a massive leg up not only with your options trading but also with directional trading.

TRENDS

In theory spotting, a trend is simple enough. Look left to right and if the price is headed up or down, it's a trend. Well, sometimes it is that simple. However, for the majority of the time you have both with and counter-trend forces operating in the market. It is possible to have long counter-trend reactions within a larger trend and sometimes, depending on the time frame you're in, these counter-trend reactions take up the majority of your screen space.

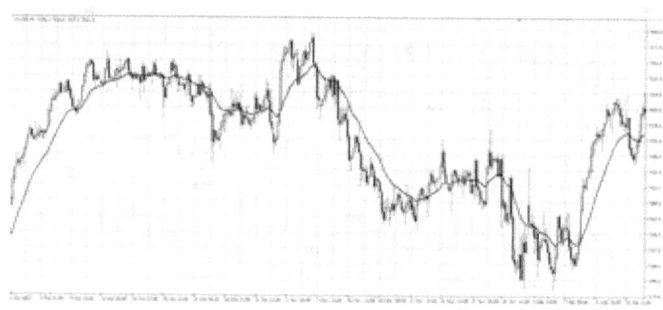

Figure 1: Trend vs Range

Take figure 1 for example. This is a chart of the UK100 CFD, which mimics the FTSE 100, on the four-hour time frame. Three-quarters of the chart is a downtrend and the last quarter is a wild uptrend. Using the looking left to the right guideline, we'd conclude that this instrument is in a range. Is that true though?

Just looking at that chart, you can see that short-term momentum is bullish. So if you were considering taking a trade on this, would you implement a range strategy or a trending one? This is exactly the sort of thing that catches traders up.

The key to deciphering trends is to watch for two things: counter-trend participation quality and turning points. Let's tackle counter-trend participation first.

COUNTER TREND PARTICIPATION

When a new trend begins, the market experiences extremely imbalanced order flow which is tilted towards one side. There's isn't much counter-trend participation against this seeming tidal wave of trend orders. Price marches on without any opposition and experiences only a few hiccups.

As time goes on though, the trend forces run out of steam and have to take breaks to gather themselves. This is where counter-trend traders start testing the trend and trying to see how far back into the trend they can go. While it is unrealistic to expect a full reversal at this point, the quality of the correction or pushback tells us a lot about the strength distribution between the with and counter-trend forces.

Eventually, the counter-trend players manage to push so far back against the trend that a stalemate results in the market. The with and counter-trend forces are equally balanced and thus the trend comes to an end. After all, you need an imbalance for the market to tip one way or another and balanced order flow is only going to result in a sideways market.

While all this is going on behind the scenes, the price chart is what records the push and pull between these two forces. Using the price chart, we can not only anticipate when a trend is coming to an end but also how long it could potentially take before it does. This second factor, which helps us estimate the time it could take, is invaluable from an options perspective, especially if you're using a horizontal spread strategy.

Here's what you look out for to gauge counter-trend participation:

Quality of counter-trend candles-Are they strong/ weak/have wicks/small-bodied, etc.?

The number of counter-trend candles within the movement-Is this changing over time?

Is the length of pushbacks-Are the pushbacks increasing in number? Are they lasting for longer?

In all cases, the greater the number of them, the greater the counter-trend participation in the market. The closer a trend is to end, the greater the counter-trend participation. Thus, the minute you begin to see price move into a large, sideways move with an equal number of buyers and sellers in it, you can be sure that some form of redistribution is going on.

Mind you, the trend might continue or reverse. Either way, it doesn't matter. What matters is that you know the trend is weak and that now is probably not the time to be banking on-trend strategies.

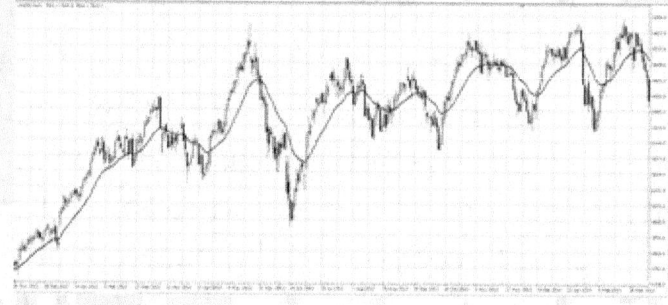

Figure 2: Counter Trend Participation

In figure 2, we can see how to counter-trend participation changes over time on the FTSE. Starting from the left, we can see that there are close to no counter-trend bars, bearish in this case, and the bulls make easy progress. Note the angle with which the bulls proceed upwards.

Then comes the first major correction and the counter-trend players push back against the last third of the bull move. Notice how strong the bearish bars are and note their character compared to the bullish bars.

The bulls recover and push the price higher at the original angle and without any bearish presence, which seems odd. This is soon explained as the bears' slam price back down and for a while, it looks as if they've managed to form a V top reversal in the trend, which is an extremely rare occurrence.

The price action that follows is a more accurate reflection of the power in the market, with both bulls and bears sharing chunks of the order flow, with overall order flow in the bull's favor but only just. Price here is certainly in an uptrend but looking at the extent of the bearish pushbacks, perhaps we should be on our guard for a bearish reversal. After all, order flow is looking pretty sideways at this point.

So how would we approach an options strategy with the chart in the state it is in at the extreme right? Well, for one, any strategy that requires an option beyond the near month is out of the question, given the probability of it turning. Secondly, looking at the order flow, it does seem to be following a channel, doesn't it?

While the channel isn't very clean, if you were aggressive enough, you could consider deploying a collar with the strike prices above and below this channel to take advantage of the price movement. You could also employ some moderately bullish strategies as price approaches the bottom of this channel and figuring out the extent of the bull move is easier thanks to you being able to reference the top of the channel.

As price moves in this channel, it's all well and good. Eventually, though, we know that the trend has to flip. How do we know when this happens?

TURNING POINTS

As bulls and bears struggle over who gets to control the order flow, price swings up and down. In figure 2, we can see several swings where the bulls pushed the bears, and the price, back upwards to maintain the uptrend. You will notice that every time price comes back into the 6427-6349 zone, the bulls seem to step in en masse and repulse the bears.

This tells us that the bulls are willing to defend this level in large numbers and strongly at that. Given the number of times the bears have tested this level, we can safely assume that above this level, bullish strength is a bit weak. However, at this level, it is as if the bulls have retreated and are treating this as a sort of last resort, for the trend to be maintained. You can see where I'm going with this.

If this level were to be breached by the bears, it is a good bet that a large number of bulls will be taken out. In martial terms, the largest army of bulls has been marshaled at this level. If this force is defeated, it is unlikely that there's going to be too much resistance to the bears below this level.

This zone, in short, is a turning point. If price breaches this zone decisively, we can safely assume that the bears have moved in and control the majority of the order flow.

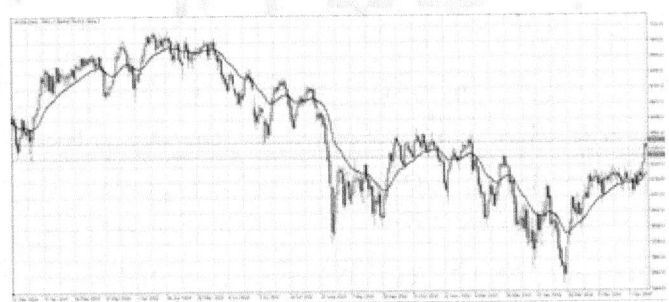

Figure 3: Turning Point Breached

Figure 3 shows us the eventual order flow as the trend turns. The decisive turning point zone is marked by the two horizontal lines and the price touches this level twice more and is repulsed by the bulls. Notice how the last bounce before the level breaks produces an extremely weak bullish bounce and price simply caves through this. Notice the strength with which the bears breakthrough.

For now, we can conclude that as long as the price remains below the turning point, we are bearishly biased. Given the amount of bullish participation in figure 3, we can safely assume that the bear trend will get reversed soon as well. You can see this by looking at the angle with which bulls push back as well as, the lack of strong bearish participation on the push upwards.

This doesn't mean we go ahead and pencil in a bull move and start implementing strategies that take advantage of the upcoming bullish move. Remember, nothing is for certain in the markets. Don't change your bias or strategy until the turning point decisively breaks.

Some key things to note here are that a turning point is always a major S/R level. It is usually a swing point where a large number of trend forces gather to support the trend. In figure 3, we have a situation where the turning point for the bull trend is the same as the one for the ensuing bear trend. This will not always be the case, so don't make the mistake of hanging on to older turning points.

The current order flow and price action are what matters the most, so pay attention to that above all else. We can safely designate the same level in figure 3 as the bearish turning point as well because this level gets tested multiple times and each time, the bears repulse the bulls back down. Also, note how the candles that test this level all have wicks on top of them.

This indicates that the bears are quite strong here and that any subsequent attack will be handled the same way until the levee breaks. Do we know when the level will break? Well, we can't say with any accuracy. However, we can estimate the probability of it breaking.

The latest upswing has seen very little bearish pushback, comparatively speaking, and the push into the level is strong. Instinct would say that there's one more rejection left here. However, who knows? Until the levee breaks, we stay bearish. When the levee breaks, we switch to the bullish side.

PUTTING IT ALL TOGETHER

So now we're ready to put all of this together into one coherent package. Your analysis should always begin with determining the current state of the market. Ranges are pretty straightforward to spot, and they occur either within big pullbacks in trends or at the end of trends.

Trends vary in strength depending on the amount of counter-trend participation they have. The way to determine counter-trend participation levels is to simply look at the price bars and compare the counter-trend ones to the trendy ones. The angle with which the trend progresses is a great gauge as well, for its strength, with steeper angles being stronger.

Next, you need to determine the turning point of the trend. The turning point is a level that is extremely well defended by the trend players and will be attacked repeatedly by the counter-trend traders in long trends. Determining a good turning is a question of reading the support and resistance.

Once you have the turning point figured out, you need to then stick to your bias and let the S/R guide you with regards to striking prices for your options strategies. Reading support and resistance is an essential skill you must master.

Conclusion

So here we are at the end of this book. We've now covered ten profitable options strategies you can use across all markets, including two powerful strategies you can use where you don't need to be concerned with which way the market will move. We've looked at strategies where you can generate steady income on an existing position, completely risk-free.

Of course, with options, it is not necessary to get into a situation where you "lose your shirt," because you can start trading options by only spending a few hundred dollars. This means you can take small risks and build up your account slowly. There are some losses, even the best traders experience losses. But, if you proceed carefully, you will learn how to trade effectively, and you can rack up more wins than losses.

Your analysis should always begin with the technical market situation which is the order flow distribution and the trend or range situation. Often you will deal with trends with close to equal participation from both sides of the market. This should tell you that a reversal is probably imminent, and you should adjust accordingly.

Support and resistance will play an important role in determining where you ought to place your strike prices. Remember to evaluate support and resistance levels from an order flow perspective, instead of looking at every single available level on the chart. Look at the order flow characteristics the previous time price made it there and compare it to the current order flow to get a feel for whether the level will hold or not.

Make sure you take the time to understand all the concepts covered in this book and then actually implement them in real life. If you don't put this knowledge you've gained to practice, you will forget it, and it would've all been just a waste of time. Remember to be patient, manage your risk, and keep learning more as you gain experience in the market. That's what makes a good trader.

Just remember that options trading is a serious business, but it can be fun and exciting too. There is no reason why making money has to be tedious and difficult. You can get involved at the highest levels of our economy with the best companies, by trading options. Hopefully, you will be able to ride the wave on the stock market and earn some of your profits.

www.ingramcontent.com/pod-product-compliance
Lightning Source LLC
Chambersburg PA
CBHW070530220526
45467CB00003B/927